PRECUT
BONANZA!

200 PIECED BLOCKS FROM CUT STRIPS & SHAPES

Kimberly Einmo

American Quilter's Society
P. O. Box 3290 • Paducah, KY 42002-3290
www.AmericanQuilter.com

Located in Paducah, Kentucky, the American Quilter's Society (AQS) is dedicated to promoting the accomplishments of today's quilters. Through its publications and events, AQS strives to honor today's quiltmakers and their work and to inspire future creativity and innovation in quiltmaking.

Executive Editor: Andi Milam Reynolds
Senior Editor: Linda Baxter Lasco
Graphic Design: Lynda Smith
Copy Editor: Elaine Brelsford
Cover Design: Michael Buckingham
Photography: Charles R. Lynch

Additional copies of this book may be ordered from the American Quilter's Society, PO Box 3290, Paducah, KY 42002-3290, or online at www.AmericanQuilter.com.

Text ©2012, Author, Kimberly Einmo
Artwork ©2012, American Quilter's Society

Library of Congress Cataloging-in-Publication Data

Einmo, Kimberly.
  Precut bonanza! : 200 pieced blocks from cut strips and shapes / by Kimberly Einmo.
     pages cm
  Summary: "Reference guide to piecing precut fabric, whether purchased or cut from your stash! Follow Kimberly's easy method of using simple, basic units such as squares, half-square triangles, four-patch units, and more to create more complex units and blocks. Pattern instructions for 3 sampler quilts, a gallery for inspiration, and Kimberly's familiar tips"--Provided by publisher.
  ISBN 978-1-60460-026-1
  1. Patchwork--Patterns. 2. Quilting--Patterns. I. Title.
  TT835.E449 2012
  746.46--dc23
                                    2012023765

DEDICATION

I dedicate this book to the three most important men in my life: my devoted husband and best friend, Kent, and our two handsome sons, Joshua and Andrew. I treasure each day because I get to share my life with the three of you. I love you all more than words can say. Thank you from the bottom of my heart for your support, encouragement, and for always knowing how to make me laugh. God has blessed my life beyond all measure!

I would also like to acknowledge the many talented, wonderful students I have met throughout the years. I'm so lucky my career allows me to meet and interact with so many gifted and amazing people. There has never been a time when I've taught a class that I haven't come away rejuvenated and uplifted by the time I spent getting to know you all. Thank you for sharing your stories and bits of your lives with me!

FUN FACT!

Our family has traveled to more than thirty-eight countries together and we have no plans of stopping! But of all the countries, world-famous cities, and forty-four states in the United States we've visited, it wasn't until November, 2011, that we took a trip to New York City! Our picture was taken on top of the Empire State Building.

To find out more fun facts and follow me as I travel around the globe, please visit my blog on my website: www.kimberlyeinmo.com.

KIMBERLY'S CREED

I love life—everything it has to offer and the endless possibilities of each new day. I especially love to quilt and to share my passion and enthusiasm for quilting with everyone!

ACKNOWLEDGMENTS

There are many people who have helped to make this book possible and I simply cannot begin to adequately express my heartfelt gratitude!

First and foremost, I want to thank my husband, Kent, our sons, Josh and Andrew, and my family. Without their continued support, encouragement, and patience, I simply couldn't have written another book.

I would like to sincerely thank my very dear friend Birgit Schüller, for sharing her unequaled and amazing talent with me by quilting so many of the quilts in this and previous books as well. She is a tour-de-force in the longarm machine community and has won countless major awards in the United States and internationally for her artistry and unparalleled creative vision. Quite simply, my quilt designs wouldn't sparkle and dazzle like they do without the addition of her thread artistry. I am very fortunate not only because she shares her talents with me through her quilting but also because I treasure her as my true friend.

I'd like to recognize and thank my dear quilting friends: Carolyn Archer, Carla Conner, Christine LaCroix, Claire Neal, Ilona Baumhofer, Judy Schrader, and Miriam Fay. These amazing, ultra-talented ladies have been a large part of the team behind many of the quilts in this and my previous books. These gals have road tested patterns, offered advice, shared ideas, and stitched their hearts out to help me get the job done and meet deadlines. Most importantly, their true friendship is the best gift of all! I'd love to introduce them to you personally (through the virtual world), so please stop by my website at: www.kimberlyeinmo.com to meet them!

I would also like to thank my dear friend Beth Russell. Beth and I met at Miami University in 1982 where we were roommates. We've remained in touch by phone and email on an almost weekly basis since then and she has been a steadfast and guiding force for me all these years. I'm so blessed to have a friend such as her.

I'd like to sincerely thank my publisher, Meredith Schroeder, my talented editors, Andi Reynolds and Linda Lasco, graphic designer Lynda Smith, and all the many creative and talented people at the American Quilter's Society. They have, yet again, transformed my manuscript so exquisitely into another gorgeous and professional publication. I am sincerely grateful for my association with them since 2004. They are like my extended family. Thank you all so much!

A huge thank you to the following folks for their very generous support for supplying the beautiful fabrics, threads, and batting used to make most of the quilts in this book:

Kyle Sanchez, Robert Kaufman Fabrics
Lissa Alexander, Moda Fabrics/United Notions
Tricia Santamaria, Fairfield Processing Corporation
Dario Valtorta, Aurifil Threads

I'd like to thank the ultra-talented gal behind the camera who took many of the photos you see in this book, Alisha Pergola. She is able to capture through her lens what I see in my mind's eye so brilliantly. Thank you, Alisha!

CONTENTS

INTRODUCTION

When Jelly Rolls first hit the scene in 2006, who could have possibly imagined they would still be the hottest ticket in quiltmaking these many years later? Not only have they stuck around, but they gave birth to a whole new genre in the quilting world known as "precuts." Those first 2½" strip rolls led to the creation of other fabric packs including Layer Cakes, Charm Squares, and so much more!

Since I began using Jelly Rolls to create the quilts for my second book, *Jelly Roll Quilts & More*, followed by a new set of exciting designs for my third book, *Jelly Roll Quilt Magic*, I still believe I've only touched the tip of the iceberg of creative design potential using precuts to make dazzling quilts.

Quite simply, the creative power of precuts is endless!

And really, what's not to love? Precuts offer so much bang for your buck—and in these tough economic times, we need all the help we can get. As quilters, most of us must be frugal not only with our finances but also with our time. There are so many distractions and commitments in our daily lives that our quilting time can easily get chipped away while we juggle other priorities. Family. Work. Continuing education. Career paths. Time spent on the computer (note to self: time spent on the Internet can be quite a time-waster!). Charitable work. Social obligations. It's no surprise I hear more and more from my students and quilting friends they just don't have as much time to spend quilting as they once did. So the time they do spend creating becomes even more precious. But I have a fabulous solution.

Let me introduce you to the wonderful world of Modular Quilting.

When I began designing and constructing blocks using precuts, I discovered I was cutting the same basic units repeatedly—squares, rectangles, triangles, and so on. However, when I realized that I rarely made any ⅛" cuts, I had one of those "light bulb" moments: I realized the concept of working with quarter-, half-, and whole-size pieced units is similar to those ultra-popular, mix-and-match closet storage systems and to modern architecture and design. I call this type of block construction using precut units MODULAR QUILTING.

Simply put, Modular Quilting is piecing using whole-, half-, and quarter-inch increments to construct simple, basic units. Nothing could be easier or more fun! And this new concept is something quilters of all skill levels can enjoy while reaping instant gratification. All it takes are some basic building blocks and a desire to dive right in to cut and stitch!

A quick search of the definition of modular design resulted in this: *to organize a complex system as a set of components that can be developed and utilized independently and then plugged together.* That makes perfect sense, doesn't it? With that in mind:

Modular Quilting is a system of simple, pieced units used to create new blocks, settings, or complex-looking designs.

This book is a guide to Modular Quilting and the ULTIMATE REFERENCE GUIDE FOR PRECUTS.

So there you have it. If you can master a few basic cutting and piecing techniques, combined with some time-saving and accurate methods, you can design your own dazzling quilts in a minimal amount of time while saving money!

That's it in a nutshell. Using precut fabric bundles (whether you buy them pre-made or make your own from your stash) is the key to creating easy yet dynamic quilts! I hope you'll refer to this book over and over again for ideas, tips, time-saving tricks, and for unlimited inspiration. More than anything, I hope the hours you spend creating are fun and stress-free. So, let's get started. Are you ready?

This brand new concept of Modular Quilting for today's quilters is an idea whose time has come. And it is for YOU!

Prepare to play with your precuts and scraps.

I believe most quilters know what Jelly Rolls and precut fabric bundles are by now. Whenever I'm teaching or lecturing for quilt guilds or at large quilt shows around the country, I always ask by a show of hands how many people actually own a Jelly Roll. Most people in the audience raise their hands. Then I ask that same group how many of them have actually untied the bow and removed the rubber band holding those strips together in a roll and not nearly as many hands go up! So while people may love to buy (and collect) these 2½" strip fabric rolls, once they get them home and into their sewing rooms, they aren't quite sure what to do with them. That's where this book comes in. Let me tell you why there is truly so much to love about them:

• Each roll that contains 40 – 2½" strips is equivalent to 2½ yards of fabric!
• They are an economical way to sample each design from a fabric line.
• 2½" strips are the most versatile strip width used in quiltmaking.
• Rolls and precut bundles are completely portable and easy to tote.
• They store easily and neatly in your stash.
• They offer limitless design opportunities!
• Much of the cutting is done so you can dive right into your project and get to the good stuff!
• Your quilts will be ultra scrappy yet beautifully coordinated.
• Quite simply, they are just so much fun to collect!

Have a stash? Use a stash!

As much as I love to buy new Jelly Rolls, Roll-Ups, Charm Packs, and Layer Cakes, like many of you, I already have a huge stash of fabric at home. So why not do some serious stash busting and use up those fabrics you bought a decade ago that have been languishing in your drawers or on your shelves for all these years? I'll bet you have fabric squirreled away in boxes or places you have completely forgotten about. (Ask me how I know.) So it's time for all those textile lovelies to see the light of day again. Here are some great ideas as to how to effectively use your stash or scrap fabrics to create your own bundles:

• Easily convert scraps, fat quarter bundles, and other odd yardage amounts to precut sizes—2½" strips, 5" and 10" squares, and so on.
• Tackle the task in small amounts. Take one color, one filled drawer or box, or one group of fabrics at a time and cut them into strips. This way it won't seem as overwhelming as trying to do it all at once!
• Host a stash-busting swap party with a few friends.
• Trade strips with your friends; increase the variety of fabrics but not the amount you have to store.
• Start a strip stash! Cut one or two 2½" strips from each new fabric you buy before it goes into your stash.
• Start a stash of 10" squares. Cut your fabrics into 10" squares and store them in a small unused pizza box or plastic bin.
• Ask your local quilt shop if they will cut 2½" strips for you (During slow times, be considerate!) or if you might rent time on their die-cutting machine.

Most of us have one of these—*a STASH of fabrics just waiting to be cut up and put to good use!*

Outdated fabrics in your stash? There's no such thing with precuts!

Use the outdated or "old" fabrics in your stash. Believe me when I tell you those not-so-stylish fabrics will make your quilts sparkle with excitement! The truth is, those fabrics that were so "in fashion" in the 1990s (or possibly decades earlier) probably don't look as appealing to you now. Am I right?

Here's the great news: if you cut those out-dated fabrics into 2½" strips, or 5" squares, you'll not only reduce the bulk in your closets and drawers, but more importantly, those fabrics will look new again when you merge them with the fabrics from your precut bundles. And it takes almost no time at all to make your own new collection of fabrics. Here are some great categories to group your fabrics if you're going to make your own or add to your existing precut bundles:

- Brights
- Batiks
- Holiday
- Monochromatic
- Country
- Reproduction
- Juvenile
- Theme

KIMBERLY'S TOP TIP

I've shared it before, but this tip is just too good not to mention again. Have you ever untied the bow from your Jelly Roll strips only to have a zillion little fabric sprinkles explode all over your clothes and the room? It can be a mess! Here's what to do: Use a sticky-tape lint roller and roll it repeatedly over the top and bottom of your strip bundle *before* you untie and unroll the strips. You may need to use several sheets of tape, but this simple action will reduce the fabric crumbs by at least 80%! Simple, yet so effective. Trust me, this really works. It's one of my best tips for working with Jelly Rolls and precuts!

STEP 2 – LET'S GET STARTED

How to use this book

I'm sure you know by now that this isn't a traditional book of quilt projects. This is a personal reference manual for designing your own unique, fabulous quilts using 2½" strip rolls, precut fabric bundles, or your stash! This is fundamentally so easy to do. Simply learn how to construct a few basic quilting units, then combine them in an infinite number of ways to create intricate-looking blocks. Before you know it, you'll be on your way to becoming a quilt-designing diva while having fun in the process!

This book is the ultimate guide for precuts. Whether you are a true beginner or an advanced quilter, you'll find everything you need to know about making stunning quilts from these amazing fabric bundles or your scrap basket. My personal goal for you is simple: I want to save you time, money, frustration, and provide you with as many tips and tricks as I can to make the process of creating quilts from precuts fun.

Here's what you'll need:

A place to sew	Whether you have a lovely studio or you share a room in your home with your family, find a place to set up your sewing machine, cutting mat, and ironing station so you can work in comfort.
A good chair	Proper support for your back is essential, so a great chair is a good investment.
Good lighting	Try to use natural light whenever possible and supplement with full spectrum artificial light so you won't strain your eyes.
Sewing machine in good working condition	Have your machine serviced regularly for hours of frustration-free stitching. Treat it to a "spa day" with a licensed technician at least once a year. Clean the bobbin housing area every time you change the bobbin.
¼" piecing foot	For true accuracy I recommend having two piecing feet: one with a ¼" guide and one without.
Rotary cutter	Use at least a size 45mm rotary cutter, but if possible have a 60mm cutter as well.
Rotary blades	It is imperative to have a new, sharp blade in your rotary cutter, with spare blades on hand to replace it whenever it becomes dull or gets a nick and skips threads.
Self-healing rotary cutting mat	Use a mat that isn't warped or deeply grooved from hours (years!) of use. Choose a mat *with* measurement lines. Remember—they put those lines on the mat for a reason. Measure twice, cut once!
Machine needles	Keep a variety of needle sizes on hand, but use a size 75/10 quilting needle for piecing.
Iron	Use an iron with plenty of steam and keep the soleplate clean.
Ironing surface	A sturdy ironing board is essential. One that adjusts to fit your height is a blessing.
Fabric	Use quilt-shop-quality 100-percent cotton fabric.
Thread	Use a 50-wt. cotton thread in a neutral color for piecing.
Batting	I prefer low-loft, natural fiber batting such as bamboo, cotton, or wool. Choose your favorite.

Scissors	Keep sharp shears on hand and small snips for clipping threads.
Seam ripper	Use a seam ripper with a sharp point. Discard your old, broken, or rusty rippers. Really, it is okay to throw them out. New seam rippers are inexpensive!
Specialty rulers	These specialty tools make cutting and stitching the units in this book very easy.
Acrylic rulers	You'll need a 6" x 24" acrylic ruler and a 12" square ruler at the very least.
Straight pins	The long, flat, flower-head pins work the best.
Marking tools	A Hera™ Marker, mechanical pencil, disappearing blue ink pen, and rolling chalk markers are very helpful to have on hand.
Basting tools	Basting safety pins or a basting gun work well.
Basic sewing supplies	Keep a fully stocked sewing box or bin full of basic sewing supplies handy.

Abbreviations you need to know to use this book:

HST – half-square triangle unit	**RSU** – right side up
QST – quarter-square triangle unit	**RSD** – right side down
RST – right sides together	**WST** – wrong sides together
LOF – length of fabric	**WOF** – width of fabric

KIMBERLY'S TOP TIP

Have you ever seen a fabric line you absolutely love but the shop or online source only carries a Layer Cake and not a Jelly Roll? Buy the Layer Cake! Here's what you may not know: a 10" square cut into four 2½" strips is the equivalent of one 2½" Jelly Roll strip! Inch for inch, a Layer Cake is equivalent to a Jelly Roll bundle—2½ yards of fabric.

Precut	Measurement	Total Yardage (approximate)	
Fat Quarter	18" x 22"	Equals ¼ yard	
Jelly Roll – 40 strips	2½" x 42"	Equals 2¾ yards	
Honey Bun – 40 strips	1½" x 42"	Equals 1⅔ yards	
Layer Cake – 40 squares	10" x 10"	Equals 2½ yards	
Charm Squares	5" x 5"	Depends on the number of squares per pack	
Turnover	6" half-square triangle units	Depends on the number of triangles per pack	
Dessert Roll – 20 strips	5" x 42"	Equals 2½ yards	
Candy Bars – 40 rectangles	2½" x 5"	Equals ⅓ yard	
Petit Fours – 40 squares	2½" x 2½"	Equals less than ¼ yard	

STEP 3 – MASTERING THE BASICS

Welcome to the world of Modular Quilting!
If you can master a few fundamental rotary-cutting and piecing skills, you will get the most out of your 2½" strips and precut fabric packs. It's easy, and I'll show you how! Using the concept of Modular Quilting, you can construct a wide variety of different size blocks to create an unlimited number of exciting and dynamic quilt layouts. You can make all the blocks in this book either by using some of my specialty rulers designed to save time, money, and fabric, or you can make the blocks using more traditional methods. Both methods will be reviewed in detail in this section, so I hope you'll refer to these pages whenever necessary. First, let's review some of the basic cuts and units.

Unit	Description	How to cut	Image
A	Quarter-square triangle	Cut triangles from 2½" strips using Side A of EZ Flying Geese Ruler. **OR** Cut a 5¼" square twice diagonally **OR** use the template on page 77. *You can cut these units in a variety of sizes depending on the finished size of your block.*	
B	Half-square triangle	Cut triangles from 2½" strips using Side B of EZ Flying Geese Ruler. **OR** Cut a 2⅞" square once diagonally. *You can cut these units in a variety of sizes depending on the finished size of your block.*	
C	Square	Cut squares from 1½" strips, 2½" strips, 5" or 10" squares.	
D	Rectangle	Cut rectangles measuring 1½" x 2½", 2½" x 4½", or 5" x 10".	
E	Diamond	Cut diamonds from 2½" strips using the 45-degree line and 2½" markings on the ruler.	
F	TRI Triangle	Cut triangles from fabric strips using the TRI Tool™. **OR** Use template on page 76. *You can cut these units in a variety of sizes depending on the finished size of your block.*	
G	RECS Triangle	Cut triangles from fabric strips using the RECS Tool™. **OR** Use template on page 77. *You can cut these units in a variety of sizes depending on the finished size of your block.*	

Basic unit construction • All of these units can be made in a variety of sizes based on the size of your block.

Description	How to Construct	Pieced Units
Half-Square Triangle (HST) unit	• Place two half-square triangle units RST and stitch on the long side. • Press the seam allowance toward darker triangle.	
TRI-RECS unit	• Sew RECS triangles to both sides of a TRI unit. • Press the seam allowances away from TRI unit.	
Double–Rectangle unit	• Sew two rectangles together. • Press the seam allowance toward the darker rectangle.	
Triple-Rectangle unit	• Sew 3 rectangles together. • Press the seam allowance toward the darker rectangle(s).	
Four-Patch unit	• Sew two squares together. • Press the seam allowances toward the darker squares. • Make two units; flip one unit, place RST, and sew. • Press the seam allowance to one side, or press the seam open so unit lies flat.	
Rectangle-Squares unit	• Sew 2 squares together. • Press the seam allowance toward the darker square. • Sew a rectangle to the 2-squares unit. • Press the seam allowance toward the rectangle.	
Triangles-Square unit	• Sew the short sides of 2 quarter-square triangle units to the sides of a square. • Press the seams away from the square. • Add a large triangle. • Press the seam allowance toward the large triangle.	
Flying Geese unit	• Sew a B (side triangle) to an A (center triangle), matching the notched edges and pointed edges. • Press the seam allowance toward the wing unit. • Sew a B triangle to other side of the A triangle and press the seam allowance toward the wing unit. OR • Use the traditional method (page 14).	

Description	How to Construct	Pieced Units
Triple-Triangle unit	• Sew 2 quarter-square triangle units together along the short sides. • Press the seam allowance toward the darker triangle. • Sew a half-square triangle to the quarter-triangles unit on the long side. • Press the seam allowance toward the half-square triangle.	
Stem unit	• Cut 1 – 1¼" x 5" rectangle. • Cut 1 – 2½" square once diagonally. • Sew rectangle between the 2 triangles. • Press seams toward rectangle. • Trim the ends and square up. • The unit should measure 2½" unfinished. *You can make these units in a variety of sizes depending on the finished size of your block.*	
Quad-Triangle unit	• Cut quarter-square triangle units from 1½" width strips using Side A of the EZ Flying Geese Ruler. • Sew 2 Side A triangles together along the short sides. • Press the seam allowance toward the darker triangle. • Make 2 units; place the units RST and sew. • Press the seam allowance open so unit lies flat. OR • Use 4 triangles cut twice diagonally from a 3¼" square. • The unit should measure 2½" unfinished.	
Square-in-a-Square unit	• Sew 4 – 2½" triangles to all four sides of a 3⅜" square. *(This is one of the few times you'll have to cut a fraction other than quarter- or half-inches.)* • Press the seams toward the triangles. • The unit should measure 4½" unfinished.	
Triangle-Triangle unit	• Sew two quarter-square triangle units to the sides of a half-square triangle unit on the short side. • Press the seam allowances away from the half-square triangle. • Add a large half-square triangle to the unit. • Press the seam allowance toward the large triangle.	
RECS – Rectangle Units	• Sew 2 RECS triangles together. Repeat. • Press the seam allowances toward the darker fabric. • Join the 2 RECS units together to form a square.	

Many methods. Learn the difference and choose your favorite!

I have designed a number of rulers and acrylic tools that feature my signature method of no math, no wasted fabric, and no stress techniques. These tried-and-true techniques allow quilters to get the most bang for their buck especially when using precut fabric bundles. So I've included these rulers in the instructions and feature diagrams on how to use them. I've also included an acrylic tool set that will give you more ways to expend your repertoire of units and blocks constructed from precuts (see Resources, page78).

EZ Flying Geese Ruler by Kimberly Einmo
EZ Jelly Roll Ruler by Kimberly Einmo
TRI-RECS TOOLS by Darlene Zimmerman

These specialty rulers are designed to save time, money, and fabric, but you don't have to have any of these tools! You may choose more traditional techniques to make the basic cuts and units. Study the choices, then choose your method. Let's get going!

How to make half-square triangle units (HSTs) using the EZ Flying Geese Ruler

• Place 2 fabric strips RST.
• Use the mint green Side B to cut B patches, rotating ruler as shown.(Be careful not to flip the ruler over to Side A.) NOTE: If you are right-handed, begin cutting on the left side of strip unit and cut from left to right. If you are left-handed, begin cutting on the right side of strip unit and cut from right to left.
• Keep the fabric patches RST and stitch ¼" on the long side of the triangles.
• Press the seams closed first, then press the seam allowance toward the darker fabric.
• Trim the dog ears from the end of the HST.

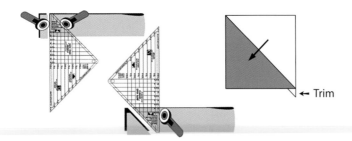

← Trim

Can you make HSTs from 2½" strips using a traditional method? Of course! Here are two easy ways.

• Place 2 – 2½" squares RST.
• Draw a diagonal line corner to corner. This is the stitching line.
• Stitch on the line. Trim ¼" away from the stitching line and discard small triangles.
• Press the unit with the seam toward the darker triangle.

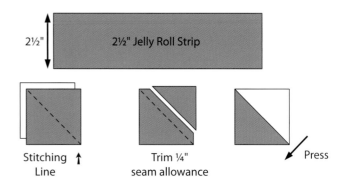

2½"   2½" Jelly Roll Strip

Stitching ↑ Line   Trim ¼" seam allowance   ↙ Press

OR

• Pair 2 different 2½" strips RST and cut a 2½" x 3¼" rectangle unit.
• Line up the 45-degree line on your ruler along the bottom of the rectangle unit and draw two diagonal lines as shown with a ½" space between the lines. One line will begin at the top left corner; the other will be drawn from the bottom right corner.These are the stitching lines.
• Stitch on the lines and cut between the lines (¼" from each stitching line).
• Press the seams toward the darker triangles.
• Each 3¼" rectangle unit will yield 2 – 2½" unfinished HST units.
• 2 – 2½" x 40" strips will yield 22 – 2½" unfinished triangles.

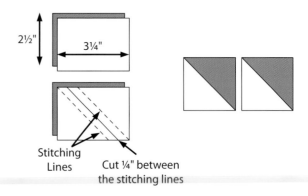

2½"   3¼"

Stitching Lines   Cut ¼" between the stitching lines

How to make Flying Geese units using the EZ Flying Geese Ruler

- Cut fabrc strips according to the finished size of the Flying Geese units shown on the left of the magenta pink Side A of the ruler. NOTE: Two or four layers of fabric strips work best. Six or more layers result in slippage and a loss of cutting accuracy.
- Use Side A to cut A triangle "geese" units (center triangles) from the strips. See the diagram on the ruler.
- Fold another fabric strip RST and use Side B to cut "wing" units (side triangles) from the strips. See the diagram on the ruler. This results in mirror-image wing units.

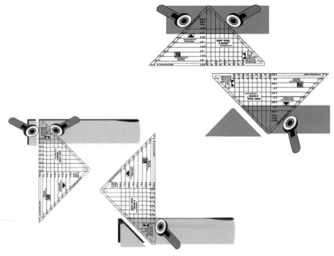

- Match notched edge to notched edge and pointed edge to pointed edge when lining up the geese and wing units. Sew a B (wing) unit to an A (goose) unit using a ¼" seam allowance.
- Press the unit closed first; then press the unit open with the seam allowance toward the wing unit.
- Sew a B triangle to other side of A unit and press the seam allowance toward wing unit. NOTE: Seam allowances must always be pressed away from center triangle! Trim "dog ears" on sides. Square up units if necessary.

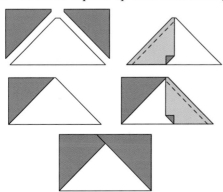

EZ Flying Geese Ruler Handy Strip Reference Chart

You'll definitely want to keep this chart handy and refer to it often. It will help you calculate the number of triangles you can cut from one strip of fabric (based on a 40" strip). Use this chart to easily convert all of your commercial patterns to cut triangles without wasting any fabric!

Strip Width	# of Triangles from Side A (quarter-square triangle units)	# of Triangles from Side B (half-square triangle units)
2½"	14	24
3"	11	22
3½"	9	20
4"	8	18
4½"	7	16
5"	7	13
5½"	6	12
6"	5	10
6½"	5	10

How to make Flying Geese units using the traditional method

- Cut 1 – 2½" x 4½" rectangle plus 2 –2½" x 2½" squares.
- Draw a diagonal line from corner to corner on the backs of the squares.
- Place one square RST on the rectangle and stitch on the line. Trim ¼" from the stitching line.
- Press the seam toward the small side triangle.
- Add the other square. Stitch, trim, and press as before.

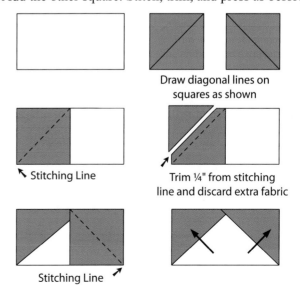

Draw diagonal lines on squares as shown

↖ Stitching Line

Trim ¼" from stitching line and discard extra fabric

Stitching Line ↗

How to use the EZ Jelly Roll Ruler

I designed my EZ Jelly Roll Ruler to work easily and efficiently with all precuts. The ruler is 5" x 10", which makes it half of a Layer Cake or any 10" square! The mint green markings show up well on all fabrics so you can cut your strips and squares into manageable units in a snap!

Can you use other rulers to rotary cut your precuts? Of course you can! But I think that once you start using this handy-dandy ruler, it will soon become your favorite "go-to" ruler for cutting precuts.

How to cut squares:

Line up the mint green highlight line along the edge of your precut strip, matching the width of your strip. Cut squares.

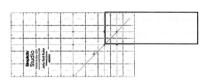
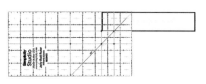

How to cut rectangles:

Line up the mint green highlight line along the edge of your precut strip matching the width of your strip.
Use the ¼", ½", or whole-inch markings to cut rectangles the desired unit size.

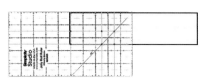

How to cut diamonds:

Line up the 45-degree line along the vertical edge of your fabric strip and trim a triangle off the end. Slide the ruler over to the cutting line to match the width of your fabric strip to cut diamonds.

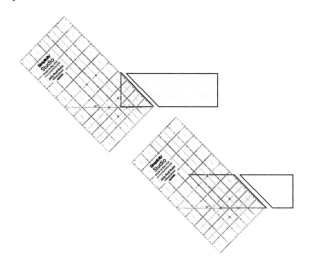

EZ Jelly Roll Ruler Handy Strip and Square Reference Table

I've included two more charts you'll definitely want to keep within easy reach for quick reference. They will help you calculate the number of basic units you can cut from strips (based on a 40" strip) and precut squares. Use this chart to easily convert all your commercial patterns to help you avoid wasting any fabric from your precuts!

Size of unit	# of units cut from a 5" square (Charm Pack)	# of units cut from a 10" square (Layer Cake)
1½" x 1½"	9	36
2½" x 2½"	4	16
2½" x 5"	2	8
5" x 5"	1	4
5" x 10"	0	2

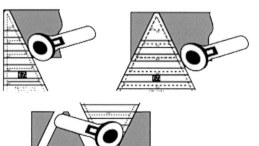
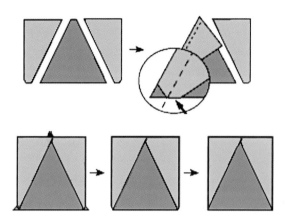
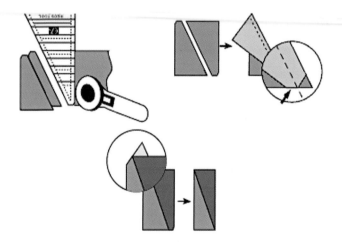

Strip Width	Unit Size	# of Units From Strip
1½"	1½" x 1½"	26
	1½" x 2"	20
	1½" x 2½"	16
	1½" x 3"	13
	1½" x 3½"	11
	1½" x 4"	10
	1½" x 4½"	8
	1½" x 5"	8
	1½" x 5½"	7
2½"	2½" x 2½"	16
	2½" x 3"	13
	2½" x 3½"	11
	2½" x 4"	10
	2½" x 4½"	8
	2½" x 5"	8
	2½" x 5½"	7

How to use the TRI RECS TOOLS

I frequently use these tools to make those pesky star points for blocks such as 54-40 or Fight. These tools are designed to work well with strips in half- and whole-inch increments so they are perfect to use with Jelly Roll strips. Once again, these specialty tools allow you to get the most out of precuts without wasting any fabric. Try them. I think you'll like them as much as I do.

• Cut fabric strips ½" wider than the finished size of TRI RECS units. Lay top edge of the TRI or REC tool along the top edge of the strip and align the bottom of the strip with the appropriate line on the tool. Cut on both sides.

• Rotate the tool and align with the strip edge and cut again.

• With RST, lay one REC triangle on the left side of the TRI triangle as shown. Align the angle on the REC triangle with the bottom of the TRI triangle. Press seam allowance toward the REC unit.

• Add a second REC unit in the same manner and press seam allowance. Trim dog ears on corners.

• To piece double-rectangle units, place two REC units RST and align the angles as shown. Stitch and press toward the darker rectangle. Trim dog ears on the corners.

Everything you need to know about triangles!

Half-square and quarter-square triangle units.

Let's review:

Triangles are the zing in blocks that make quilts dazzle with excitement! Next to the square, they are arguably the most necessary and useful of all basic quilting units. Triangles make my patchwork world sparkle. In short, I simply love triangles!

New quilters need to learn about them. Intermediate quilters need to understand them better. And even advanced quilters may need a refresher, so listen up. You may have struggled with geometry class in high school, but as a quilter you need to know the basic principles of triangles and how they affect your blocks! Triangles can behave like rowdy kids; they can act up at the most inopportune times, causing seams to curve and blocks to ripple. *Every quilter needs to understand the basic differences between half-square and quarter-square triangle units.*

To begin, let's consider the square, cut on the straight-of-grain. Cut the square once diagonally and you get two triangles. The straight-of-grain runs along the two short sides of the triangles, with the bias edge running along the long side. These triangles are half-square triangle units because both halves came from one square.

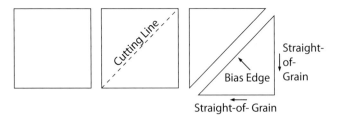

Let's consider the same square now cut twice diagonally. You get four triangles. The straight-of-grain runs along the long side of the triangle and the bias edges run along the two shorter sides. These triangles are quarter-square triangle units because four triangles came from one square.

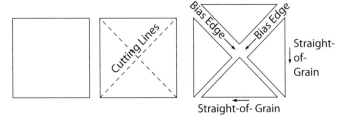

Why is this information about the bias and straight-of-grain important to you? Because every quilter needs to be aware of the placement of the bias within their blocks. The rule of thumb is that the straight-of-grain should run along the outside edge of the completed block (even though there are exceptions to this and every rule!).

Think about the setting triangles for a quilt top with blocks set on point. Corner setting triangles need the straight-of-grain on the two short sides, so cut squares once on the diagonal. Side setting triangles need the straight-of-grain on the one long side, so cut squares twice on the diagonal.

Don't be intimidated by triangles. Use them to your advantage and make your quilts spectacular!

Making a Lonestar block from 2½" strips

- Using 2½" strips, make a strip-set of fabrics #1 and #2 and a strip-set of fabrics #2 and #3.

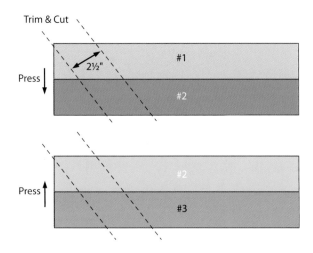

- Cut 8 diamonds, 2½" wide (page 16), from each strip set.
- Sew the diamond units together to make 8 diamond wedge units as shown.

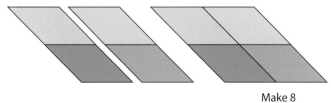

Make 8

How to construct the Lonestar without set-in seams
- Cut 4 – 5" background fabric squares once diagonally to yield 8 triangles (A triangles).
- Matching points and raw edges, sew an A triangle to a diamond wedge unit.
- Press the seam allowance toward the A triangle.
- Cut 4 – 6⅝" background fabric squares once diagonally to yield 8 triangles (B triangles).

- Line up B triangle to top raw edge of A triangle and raw edge of diamond wedge.
- Sew a B triangle to the diamond wedge unit as shown.
- Press the seam allowance toward the B triangle.
- Repeat for all 8 diamond-wedge units. There will be 4

mirror-image units.

- Sew 2 units together to form squares. Press the seam allowance open.
- True up block to 10½" unfinished.
- Join the squares into a Lonestar block.

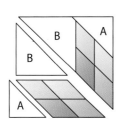
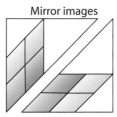
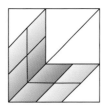

Mirror images

Note: To make one complete Lonestar, you need 4 blocks.

KIMBERLY'S TOP TIP

Here's the UPDATED truth about Lonestars – I've made literally dozens of Lonestar blocks from 2½" strips over the past few years and have taught many classes where students have made them, too. Here's the scoop about the unfinished size of Lonestar blocks: depending on a variety of factors including individual ¼" seam allowances, thread weight, needle size, your particular brand of sewing machine, and how accurately you cut, your star will end up measuring somewhere between 19" and 20½" unfinished. As for me, my stars used to consistently end up 20" unfinished, which meant I needed to adjust the next border to compensate for being short by half an inch. I've always prided myself on having very accurate ¼" seams using 40-wt. silk-covered cotton thread.

But very recently, two things changed that directly impacted the unfinished size of my Lonestar blocks. First, I began using a different ¼" piecing foot. Second, I switched to Aurifil's 50-wt. cotton thread. It was an absolute revelation to me that my unfinished Lonestar block size increased by almost a quarter inch! The thinner (stronger) thread has much less bulk and combined with the more accurate ¼" piecing foot, it made a huge

difference in the size of my blocks. So the truth is, size does matter! (Piecing foot and thread size, that is.)

However, if your Lonestar block ends up being less than 20½" unfinished, don't stress. There is an easy fix for this. You need to compensate for the size difference before you add the next border or row of blocks. Simply add an inner border with a different fabric or "extend" your block to the proper measurement with background fabric strips in the width necessary to make your unfinished block measure 20½" (or larger) and move on. No one will know the difference!

A new ¼" piecing foot and a switch to 50-wt cotton thread reduced the bulk in my seam allowance and increased my overall unfinished block size.

PHOTO TUTORIAL of how to cut and piece a perfect Lonestar

Step 1
Cut diamond pairs from strip sets.

Step 2
Match seams using a pin through both seams exactly ¼" from raw edges.

Step 3
Pin perpendicular to the straight edges of diamond units.

Step 4
Stitch to the pin and remove it when the needle is one or two stitches away. Aim the needle at the hole left by pin.

Step 5
Press the seam to one side. The point where diamond pairs meet will be perfect!

Step 6
Trim dog ears from the diamond pair units.

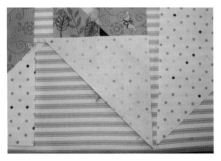

Step 7
Place an A triangle RST on the diamond unit, matching the point and two sides.

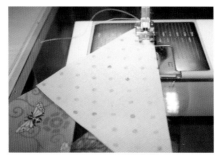

Step 8
Starting at the point, sew a scant ¼" seam.

Step 9
End stitching an the apex of the background triangle and diamond unit.

Step 10
Press the A triangle seam away from the diamond unit. Leave the dog ear at the point.

Step 11
Line up ruler using 45-degree line and 4¼" marks and carefully trim the excess from triangle A if necessary.

Step 12
Place triangle B RST on top of the diamond unit, lining up the straight edges with triangle A and the raw edge of the diamond wedge.

Step 13
Match the two sides, leaving a dog ear extending beyond the matched edges.

Step 14
Press the triangle B seam away from the diamond wedge. Trim any excess background fabric from triangle B.

Step 15
Do not trim dog ear after adding triangles A and B until the block is completely constructed.

Step 16
Join 2 wedges together to create squares.

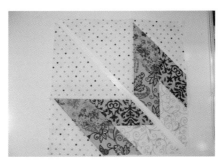

Step 17
Match the points of the diamonds and use pins in the seams to secure.

Step 18
Stitch the diamond wedges together and press the seams OPEN.

Step 19
Stitch two squares together to create half a block. Repeat. Press all seams OPEN.

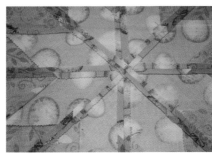

Step 20
Join the block halves together. Press the seam open as shown.

Step 21
Use a straight pin to position the points.

Step 22
Trim the remaining dog ears, being careful to leave a ¼" seam allowance for star points.

Step 23
You will have a perfect center point that lies completely flat!

How to cut a Layer Cake or 10" square

Of course there are many ways to cut a 10" square into usable units to get the most mileage from every inch of fabric. Here are some of the most commonly used cuts to make the blocks in this book.

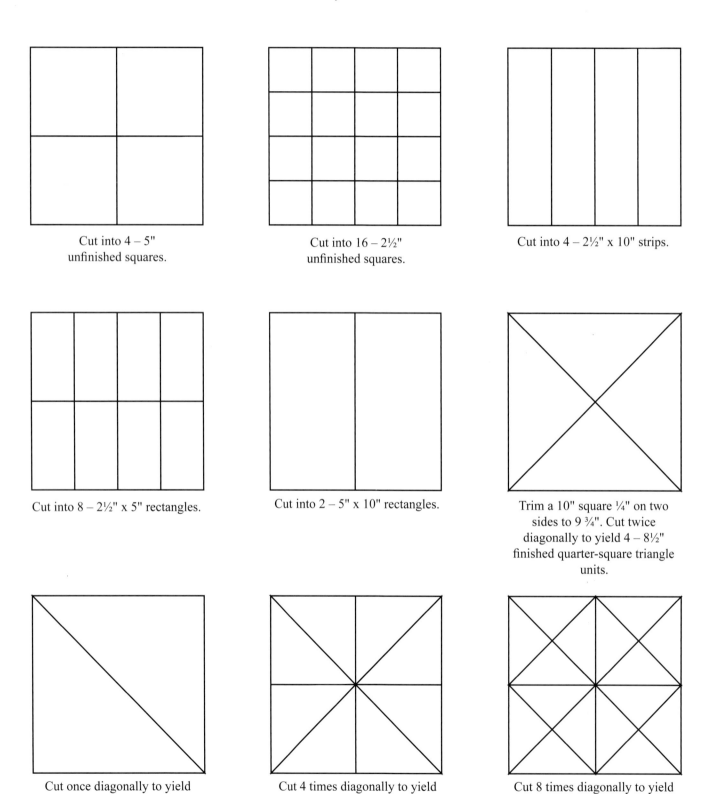

Cut into 4 – 5"
unfinished squares.

Cut into 16 – 2½"
unfinished squares.

Cut into 4 – 2½" x 10" strips.

Cut into 8 – 2½" x 5" rectangles.

Cut into 2 – 5" x 10" rectangles.

Trim a 10" square ¼" on two sides to 9 ¾". Cut twice diagonally to yield 4 – 8½" finished quarter-square triangle units.

Cut once diagonally to yield
2 – 9" finished
half-square triangle units.

Cut 4 times diagonally to yield
8 half-square triangle units.

Cut 8 times diagonally to yield
16 quarter-square triangle units.

LIBRARY OF BLOCKS: THE ULTIMATE PRECUTS BLOCKFEST!

You've mastered the basics, armed yourself with a new, sharp blade in your rotary cutter, and chosen your preferred construction methods. Now you're ready to build blocks using your precuts!

The following block library is chock-full of design ideas just waiting for you to explore. Browse through the various blocks and keep in mind that each individual block has dozens of different design options based on a number of factors including where you place the values of lights, mediums, and darks within each unit. I've included 200 different blocks, but once you multiply the creative potential of each individual block, there could be thousands of block options from which to choose!

Whenever you see SIDE A or SIDE B, it refers to using the EZ Flying Geese Ruler for cutting the triangles. The number is the measurement of the size strip you should use to make the cut. Traditional measurements are also provided.

TRY THIS!

One of my best tips for successful designing is to work in grayscale. That's right; you need to remove the color when you design. This method is especially effective when working with scrappy fabrics or precut fabric bundles. By removing the color from blocks on a design surface on your computer screen or by using just a pencil and graph paper, you will be able to visualize how the block will look in shades of black, white, and gray. If your block or quilt design looks balanced and pleasing to the eye with just shades of gray, your quilt will look terrific no matter what colors you plug in, as long as you pay attention to the value of the colors. Seriously, this works. You'll be amazed!

I encourage you to give it a try. If you use quilt design software on your computer, try using only shades of black, white, and gray to create your virtual designs. If you use good old-fashioned graph paper and pencil, you are probably already familiar with this concept. But let's take it one step further. If you'd like to see how the blocks featured in this book's block libraries might look in grayscale, simply copy them in black and white on your printer and try viewing the blocks that way. (However, this means no sharing with friends or guild members, please. Respect the publisher's copyright and my hard work as well!) When it comes time to begin cutting your fabrics, all you'll need to do is sort them by value and make sure you place them within each block where the corresponding value is placed. This works like a charm every time!

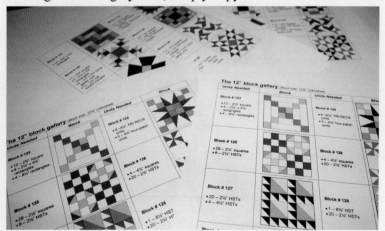

THE 6" BLOCK GALLERY
(Block size: 6½" unfinished)

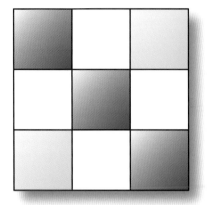

Block #1
• 9 – 2½" squares

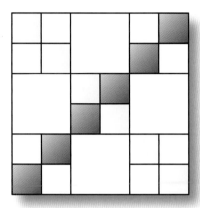

Block #2
• 4 – 2½" squares
• 5 – 2½" four-patch units

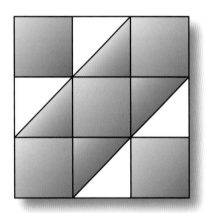

Block #3
• 5 – 2½" squares
• 4 – 2½" half-square triangle units

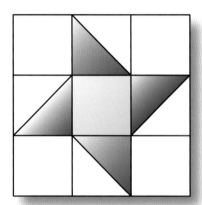

Block #4
• 5 – 2½" squares
• 4 – 2½" half-square triangle units

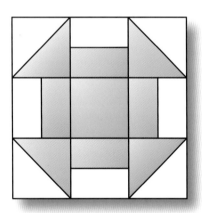

Block #5
• 1 – 2½" square
• 4 – 2½" half-square triangle units
• 4 – 2½" double-rectangle units

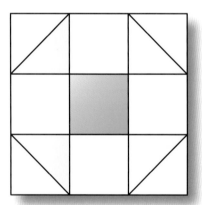

Block #6
• 5 – 2½" squares
• 4 – 2½" half-square triangle units

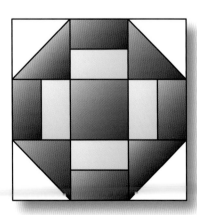

Block #7
• 1 – 2½" square
• 4 – 2½" half-square triangle units
• 4 – 2½" double-rectangle units

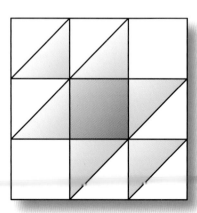

Block #8
• 3 – 2½" squares
• 6 – 2½" half-square triangle units

Block #9
- 2 – 2½" squares
- 4 – 2½" half-square triangle units
- 1 – 2½"x 6½" rectangle

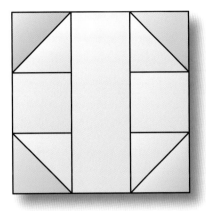

Block #10
- 1 – 2½" square
- 4 – 2½" half-square triangle units
- 4 – double-rectangle units

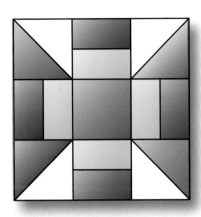

Block #11
- 9 – 2½" half-square triangle units

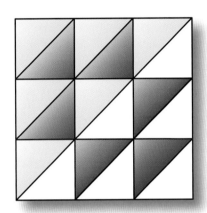

Block #12
- 9 – 2½" half-square triangle units

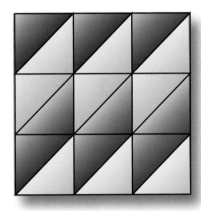

Block #13
- 9 – 2½" half-square triangle units

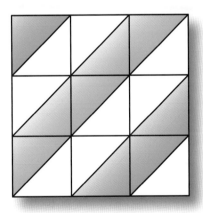

Block #14
- 3 – 2½" squares
- 6 – 2½" half-square triangle units

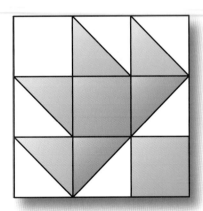

Block #15
- 5 – 2½" squares
- 4 – 2½" half-square triangle units

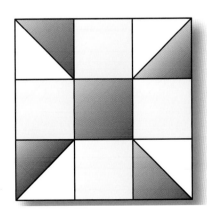

Block #16
- 5 – 2½" squares
- 4 – 2½" double-rectangle units

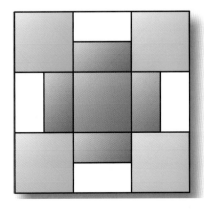

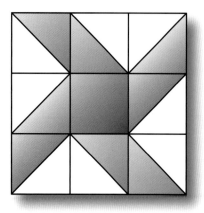

Block #17

• 1 – 2½" square

• 8 – 2½" half-square triangle units

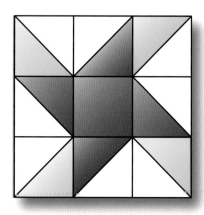

Block #18

• 1 – 2½" square

• 8 – 2½" half-square triangle units

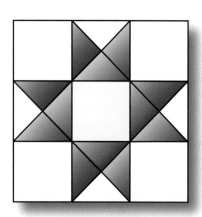

Block #19

• 5 – 2½" squares

• 4 – 2½" quad-triangle units

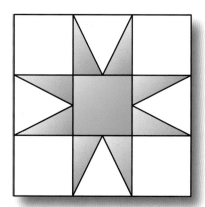

Block #20

• 5 – 2½" squares

• 4 – 2½" TRI-RECS units

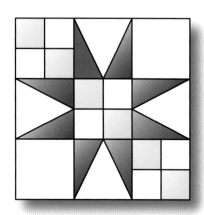

Block #21

• 2 – 2½" squares

• 3 – 2½" four-patch units

• 4 – 2½" TRI-RECS units

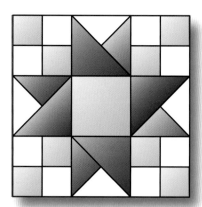

Block #22

• 1 – 2½" square

• 4 – 2½" four-patch units

• 4 – 2½" triple-triangle units

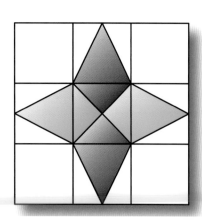

Block #23

• 4 – 2½" squares

• 4 – 2½" TRI-RECS units

• 1 – 2½" quad-triangle unit

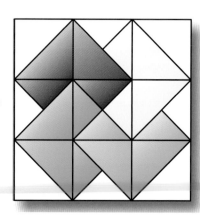

Block #24

• 1 – 2½" quad-triangle unit

• 4 – 2½" triple-triangle units

• 4 – 2½" half-square triangle units

Block #25
- 4 – 2½" squares
- 4 – 2½" half-square triangle units
- 1 – 2½" stem unit

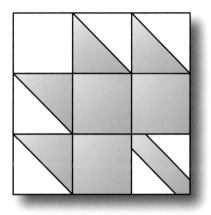

Block #26
- 3 – 2½" squares
- 4 – 2½" half-square triangle units
- 1 – 2½" stem unit
- 1 – 2½" rectangle-squares unit

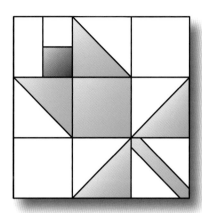

Block #27
- 6 – 2½" squares
- 3 – 2½" half-square triangle units

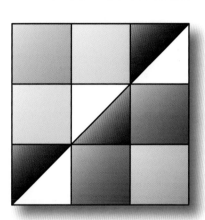

Block #28
- 1 – 2½" square
- 4 – 2½" half-square triangle units
- 4 – 2½" TRI-RECS units

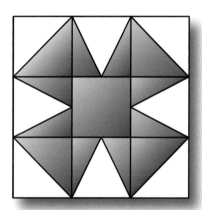

Block #29
- 9 – 2½" double-rectangle units

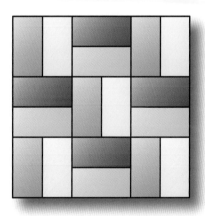

Block #30
- 4 – 2½" squares
- 5 – 2½" quad-triangle units

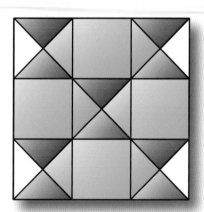

Block #31
- 7 – 2½" squares
- 2 – 2½" half-square triangle units

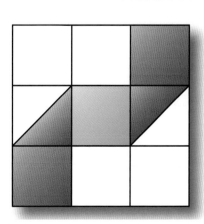

Block #32
- 1 – 2½" square
- 4 – 2½" triple-rectangle units
- 4 – 2½" quad-triangle units

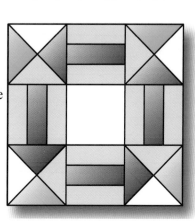

Block #33
• 4 – 2½" half-square triangle units
• 5 – 2½" four-patch units

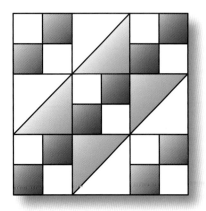

Block #34
• 8 – 2½" half-square triangle units
• 1 – 2½" quad-triangle unit

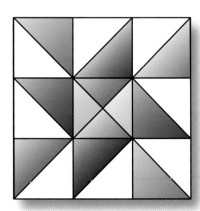

Block #35
• 1 – 2½" square
• 8 – 1½" x 2½" Flying Geese units
• 4 – 2½" half-square triangle units

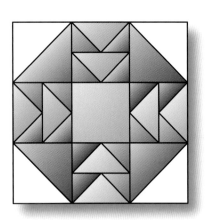

Block #36
• 4 – 2½" squares
• 1 – 2½" quad-triangle unit
• 4 – 2½" RECS-rectangle units

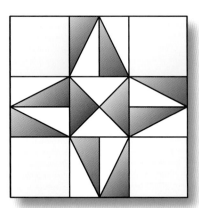

Block #37
• 1 – 2½" square
• 4 – 1½" x 2½" rectangles
• 4 – 1½" x 2½" Flying Geese units
• 4 – 2½" triangles-square units

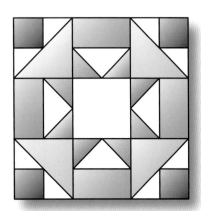

Block #38
• 1 – 2½" square
• 8 – 1½" x 2½" Flying Geese units
• 4 – 2½" double-rectangle units

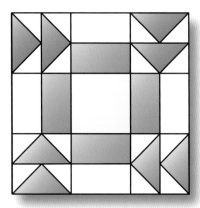

Block #39
• 1 – 2½" square
• 4 – 1½" x 2½" rectangles
• 4 – 1½" x 2½" Flying Geese units
• 4 – 2½" half-square triangle units

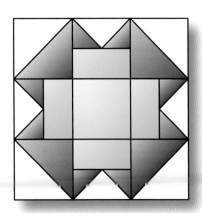

Block #40
• 1 – 2½" square
• 4 – 2½" double-rectangle units
• 4 – 2½" rectangle-squares units

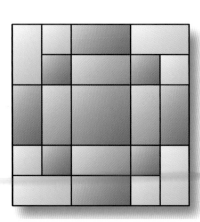

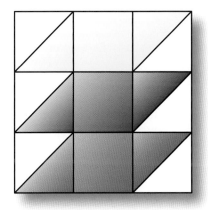

Block #41
- 3 – 2½" squares
- 6 – 2½" half-square triangle units

Block #42
- 7 – 2½" squares
- 2 – 2½" half-square triangle units

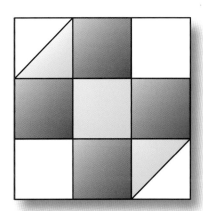

Block #43
- 6 – 2½" squares
- 2 – 2½" TRI RECS units
- 1 – 2½" quad-triangle unit

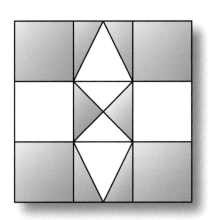

Block #44
- 8 – 2½" squares
- 1 – 2½" quad-triangle unit

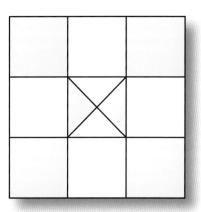

Block #45
- 1 – 2½" square
- 4 – 2½" half-square triangle units
- 4 – 2½" four-patch units

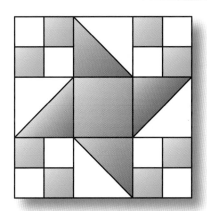

Block #46
- 1 – 2½" square
- 4 – 2½" half-square triangle units
- 4 – 2½" four-patch units

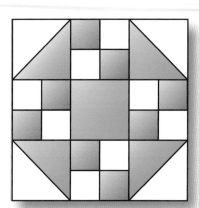

Block #47
- 5 – 2½" squares
- 4 – 2½" half-square triangle units

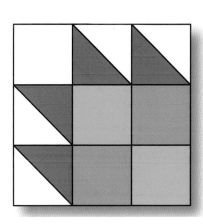

Block #48
- 5 – 2½" squares
- 4 – 1½" x 2½" rectangles
- 4 – 1½" x 2½" Flying Geese units

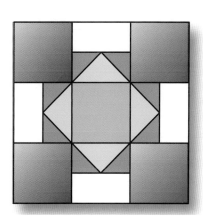

Block #49

- 1 – 2½" quad-triangle unit
- 4 – 2½" half-square triangle units
- 4 – 2½" double-rectangle units

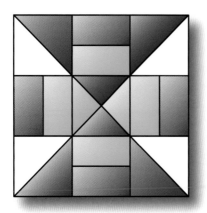

Block #50

- 4 – 2½" squares
- 4 – 2½" half-square triangle units
- 1 – 2½" quad-triangle unit

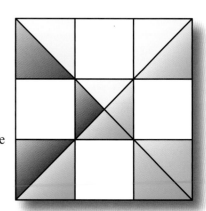

KIMBERLY'S TOP TIP

Cutting and piecing two of the tricky units for the 6" blocks

If you plan to make Block #32, you'll see it has four 2½" (unfinished) triple-rectangle units. In case you're wondering what measurement to use to cut those rectangles try this:

Cut 3 – 1¼" x 2½" rectangles

As you stitch them together, use a slightly chunky ¼" seam. (Yes, I really did just tell you to use something other than a perfect ¼" seam!) The unit may still measure a bit wider than 2½" but only slightly. If this is the case, simply square-up the units to measure 2½" x 2½" by cutting a sliver of fabric from each side. It will look just fine when sewn into the block.

You may need to trim a bit on each side to measure 2½" unfinished.

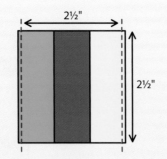

Several of the blocks in the 6" Block Gallery are constructed using tiny 1½" x 2½" Flying Geese units. They add so much visual interest and pizzazz to these blocks but admittedly, they can be quite pesky to piece because of their small size. You can use one of several methods to make these:

To use the EZ Flying Geese Ruler, simply cut 1½" wide strips for both the center triangle and the side triangles and line up the ruler in the same manner to cut the units as you would for larger sizes.

For the traditional method, cut one rectangle 1½" x 2½" and two squares 1½" x 1½" to make the Flying Geese units You may also choose to paper piece these units. Photocopy the pattern below:

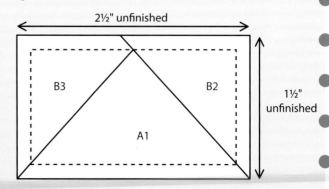

THE 8″ BLOCK GALLERY
(Block size: 8½″ unfinished)

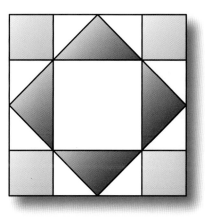

Block #51
- 1 – 4½″ square
- 4 – 2½″ squares
- 4 – 2½″ x 4½″ Flying Geese units

Block #52
- 4 – 2½″ squares
- 4 – 2½″ half-square triangle units
- 2 – 4½″ four-patch units

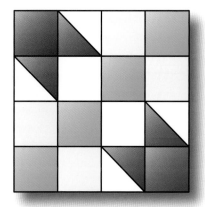

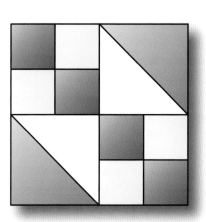

Block #53
- 2 – 4½″ four-patch units
- 2 – 4½″ half-square triangle units

Block #54
- 8 – 2½″ x 4½″ Flying Geese units

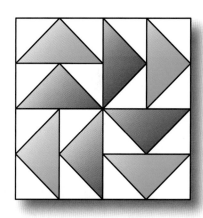

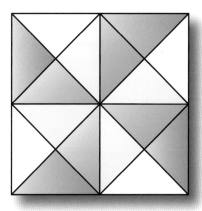

Block #55
- 4 – 4½″ quad-triangle units

Block #56
- 16 – 2½″ half-square triangle units

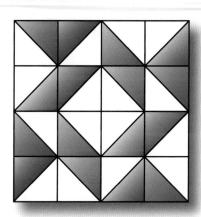

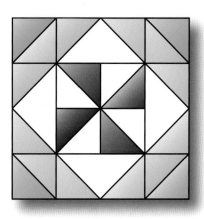

Block #57
- 8 – 2½″ half-square triangle units
- 4 – 2½″ x 4½″ Flying Geese units

Block #58
- 1 – 4½″ square
- 4 – 2½″ half-square triangle units
- 4 – 2½″ x 4½″ Flying Geese units

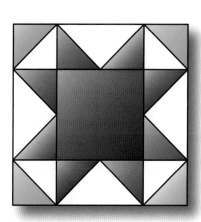

Block #59
- 1 – 4½" square
- 4 – 2½" squares
- 4 – 2½" x 4½" Flying Geese units

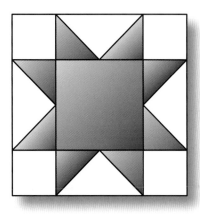

Block #60
- 4 – 2½" squares
- 1 – 4½" four-patch unit
- 4 – 2½" x 4½" Flying Geese units

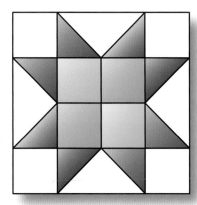

Block #61
- 4 – 4½" double-rectangle units

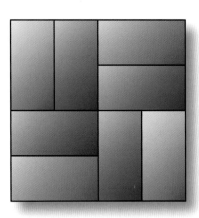

Block #62
- 8 – 2½" x 2½" half-square triangle units
- 4 – 2½" x 4½" rectangles

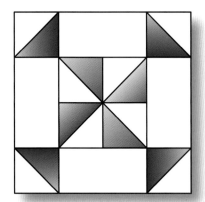

Block #63
- 4 – 2½" squares
- 12 – 2½" half-square triangle units

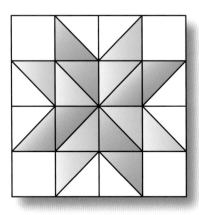

Block #64
- 4 – 4½" triple-triangle units

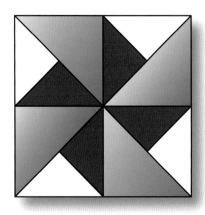

Block #65
- 16 – 2½" half-square triangle units

    OR
- 8 – 2½" x 4½" Flying Geese units

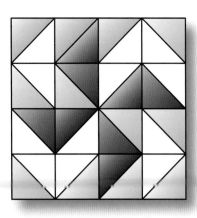

Block #66
- 16 – 2½" squares

    OR
- 4 – 4½" four-patch units

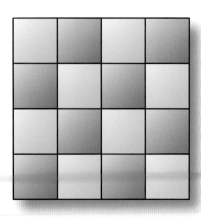

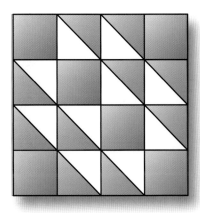

Block #67
- 6 – 2½" squares
- 10 – 2½" half-square triangle units

Block #68
- 2 – 4½" four-patch units
- 4 – 2½" squares
- 4 – 2½" four-patch units

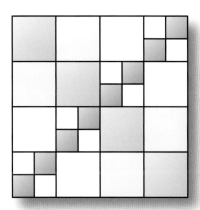

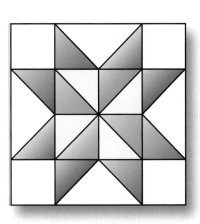

Block #69
- 4 – 2½" squares
- 4 – 2½" x 4½" Flying Geese units
- 4 – 2½" half-square triangle units

Block #70
- 4 – 2½" squares
- 6 – 2½" half-square triangle units
- 4 – 2½" Side B triangles OR 2 – 2⅞" triangles
- 2 – 4½" Side B triangles OR 2 – 4⅞" triangles

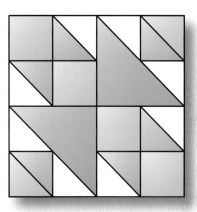

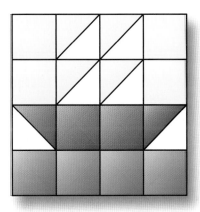

Block #71
- 10 – 2½" squares
- 6 – 2½" half-square triangle units

Block #72
- 1 – 4½" four-patch unit
- 4 – 2½" squares
- 8 – 2½" half-square triangle units

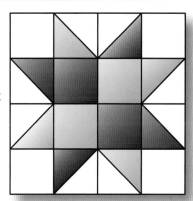

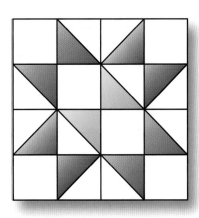

Block #73
- 6 – 2½" squares
- 10 – 2½" half-square triangle units

Block #74
- 1 – 4½" four-patch unit
- 8 – 2½" squares
- 4 – 2½" half-square triangle units

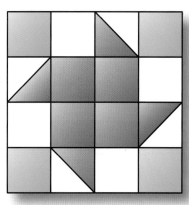

Block #75
- 16 – 2½" half-square triangle units

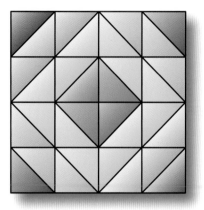

Block #76
- 2 – 2½" squares
- 10 – 2½" half-square triangle units
- 2 – 2½" x 4½" rectangles

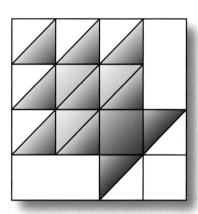

Block #77
- 16 – 2½" half-square triangle units

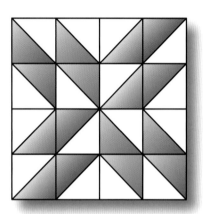

Block #78
- 16 – 2½" half-square triangle units

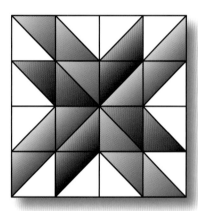

Block #79
- 8 – 2½" squares
- 8 – 2½" half-square triangle units

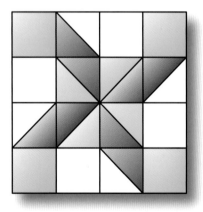

Block #80
- 4 – 4½" triple-triangle units

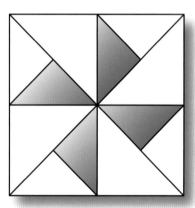

Block #81
- 8 – 2½" squares
- 8 – 2½" half-square triangle units

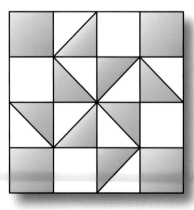

Block #82
- 4 – 2½" squares
- 2 – 2½" half-square triangle units
- 3 – 2½" side B triangles OR 3 – 2⅞" triangles
- 2 – 2½" x 4½" rectangles
- 1 – 6½" triangle OR
- 1 – 6⅞" triangle

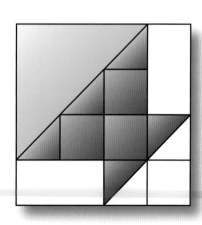

Block #83

- 16 – 2½" half-square triangle units

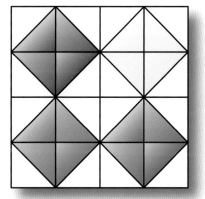

Block #84

- 8 – 2½" squares
- 8 – 2½" half-square triangle units

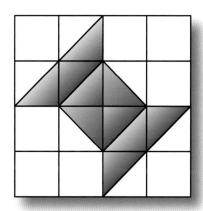

Block #85

- 16 – 2½" half-square triangle units

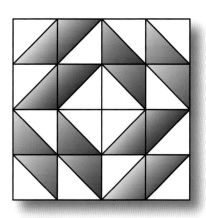

Block #86

- 1 – 4½" square-in-a-square unit
- 4 – 2½" half-square triangle units
- 4 – 2½" x 4½" Flying Geese units

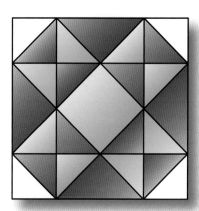

Block #87

- 4 – 2½" squares
- 1 – 4½" four-patch unit
- 4 – 2½" x 4½" rectangles

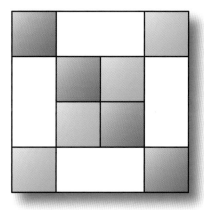

Block #88

- 1 – 4½" square-in-a-square unit
- 4 – 2½" squares
- 4 – 2½" x 4½" rectangles

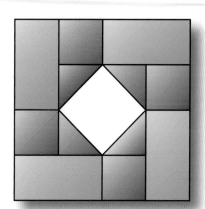

Block #89

- 1 – 4½" square-in-a-square unit
- 4 – 2½" squares
- 4 – 2½ x 4½" rectangles

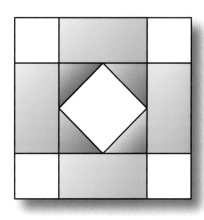

Block #90

- 12 – 2½" half-square triangle units
- 1 – 4½" half-square triangle unit

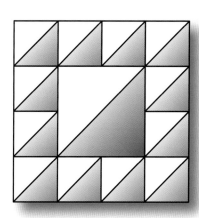

Block #91

- 1 – 4½" square-in-a-square unit
- 4 – 2½" half-square triangle units
- 4 – 2½" x 4½" Flying Geese units

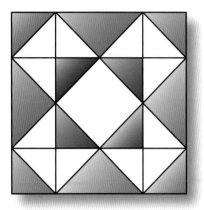

Block #92

- 16 – 2½" half-square triangle units

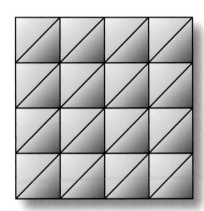

Block #93

- 1 – 4½" square-in-a-square unit
- 4 – 2½" half-square triangle units
- 4 – 2½" x 4½" Flying Geese units

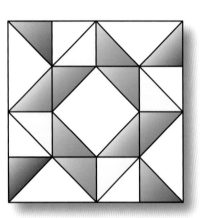

Block #94

- 8 – 2½" x 4½" Flying Geese units

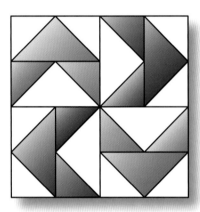

Block #95

- 1 – 4½" four-patch unit
- 12 – 2½" half-square triangle units

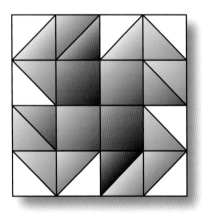

Block #96

- 1 – 4½" square
- 4 – 2½" squares
- 4 – 2½" x 4½" Flying Geese units

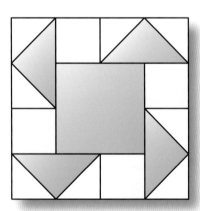

Block #97

- 16 – 2½" half-square triangle units

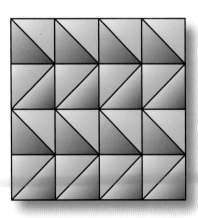

Block #98

- 1 – 4½" four-patch unit
- 4 – 2½" squares
- 8 – 2½" half-square triangle units

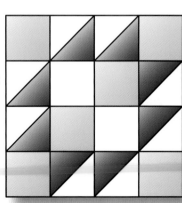

Block #99

• 16 – 2½″ half-square triangle units

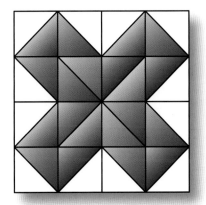

Block #100

• 6 – 2½″ x 4½″ Flying Geese units

• 4 – 2½″ half-square triangle units

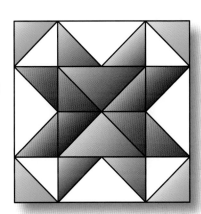

TRY THIS!

What do you do with the seemingly endless miles of binding while you're in the process of sewing it on by machine? For years, I simply wound it around my fingers into an oval "ball" and then let it sit in my lap as I tried to manage both the binding and the quilt under the needle of my machine. Ultimately, the binding would fall to the floor and end up getting stretched, or stuck under the wheel of my rolling chair, or end up in a jumbled mess with a dust bunny or two attached. Blah! Fortunately, I've discovered a better way!

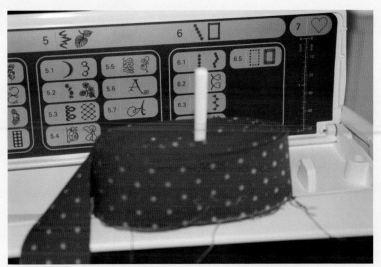

Simply place that wound binding around the empty spool holder on top of your machine. The binding will stay neat and tidy and will feed onto the quilt just perfectly. Voila!

Give it a try. It works like a charm!

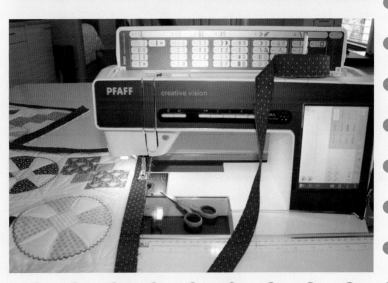

THE 10" BLOCK GALLERY
(Block size: 10½" unfinished)

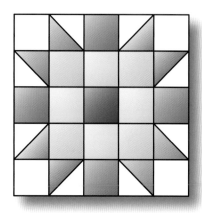

Block #101
- 17 – 2½" squares
- 8 – 2½" half-square triangle units

Block #102
- 25 – 2½" squares

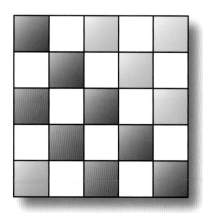

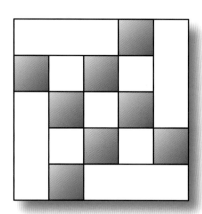

Block #103
- 13 – 2½" squares
- 4 – 2½" x 6½" rectangles

Block #104
- 1 – 6½" half-square triangle
- 16 – 2½" half-square triangle units

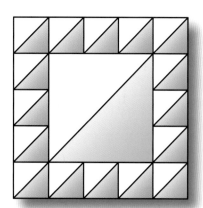

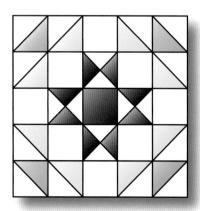

Block #105
- 9 – 2½" squares
- 12 – 2½" half-square triangle units
- 4 – 2½" quad-triangle units

Block #106
- 9 – 2½" squares
- 4 – 4½" triangle-triangle units

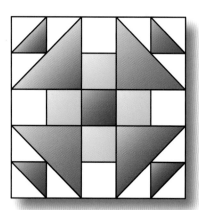

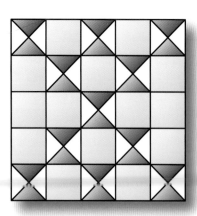

Block #107
- 14 – 2½" squares
- 11 – 2½" quad-triangle units

Block #108
- 1 – 2½" square
- 4 – 2½" x 4½" rectangles
- 4 – 4½" four-patch units

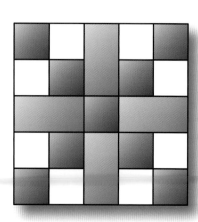

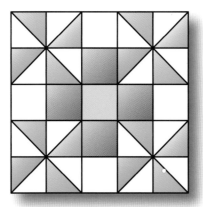

Block #109

- 9 – 2½" squares
- 16 – 2½" half-square triangle units

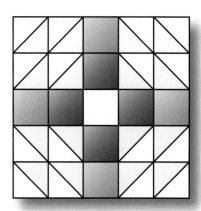

Block #110

- 9 – 2½" squares
- 16 – 2½" half-square triangle units

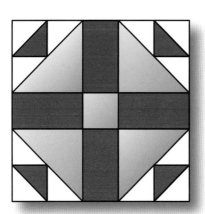

Block #111

- 1 – 2½" square
- 4 – 2½" x 4½" rectangles
- 4 – 4½" triangle-triangles units

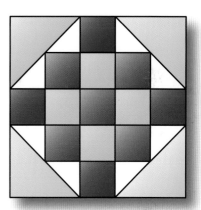

Block #112

- 9 – 2½" squares
- 4 – 4½" triangles-square units

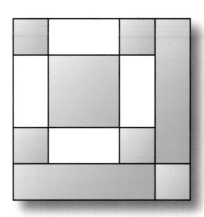

Block #113

- 1 – 4½" square
- 5 – 2½" squares
- 4 – 2½" x 4½" rectangles
- 2 – 8½" rectangles

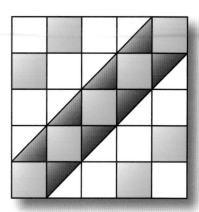

Block #114

- 9 – 2½" squares
- 2 – 4½" four-patch units
- 8 – 2½" half-square triangle units

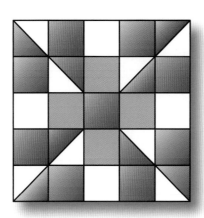

Block #115

- 17 – 2½" squares
- 8 – 2½" half-square triangle units

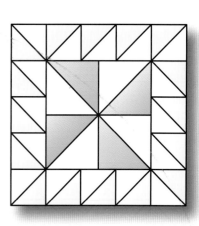

Block #116

- 16 – 2½" half-square triangle units
- 4 – 3½" half-square triangle units

Block #117

- 1 – 6½" square
- 16 – 2½" squares

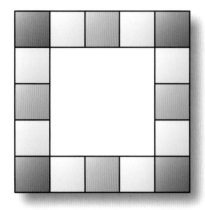

Block #118

- 1 – 2½" square
- 4 – 2½" x 4½" rectangles
- 4 – 4½" half-square triangle units

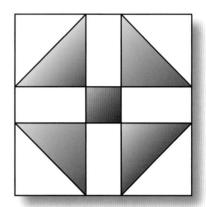

Block #119

- 13 – 2½" squares
- 4 – 2½" x 6½" rectangles

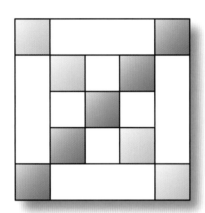

Block #120

- 9 – 2½" squares
- 12 – 2½" half-square triangle units
- 4 – 2½" quad-triangle units

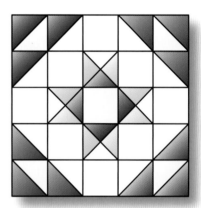

Block #121

- 1 – 6½" half-square triangle unit
- 2 – 2½" squares
- 2 – 2½" x 6½" rectangles
- 8 – 2½" half-square triangle units

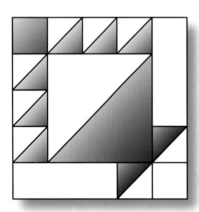

Block #122

- 1 – 6½" side B triangle OR 1 – 6⅞" triangle
- 12 – 2½" half-square triangle units
- 2 – 2½" x 6½" rectangles
- 1 – 2½" square
- 3 – 2½" Side B triangles OR 3 – 2⅞" triangles

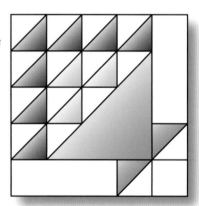

THE 12" BLOCK GALLERY
(Block size: 12½" unfinished)

Block # 123
- 12 – 2½" squares
- 4 – 2½" x 4½" rectangles
- 4 – 8½" rectangles

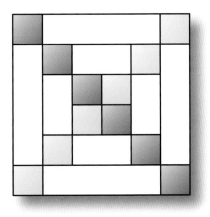

Block # 124
- 4 –4½" TRI-RECS units
- 5 – 4½" four-patch units

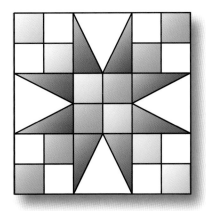

Block # 125
- 28 – 2½" squares
- 8 – 2½" half-square triangle units

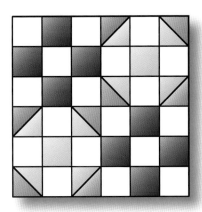

Block # 126
- 4 – 4½" squares
- 20 – 2½" half-square triangle units

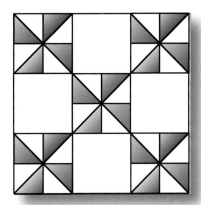

Block # 127
- 20 – 2½" half-square triangle units
- 4 – 4½" half-square triangle units

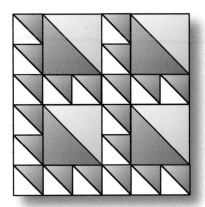

Block # 128
- 1 – 8½" half-square triangle unit
- 20 – 2½" half-square triangle units

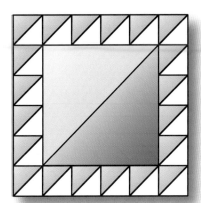

Block # 129
- 4 – 2½" squares
- 1 – 4½" square
- 4 – 2½" x 4½" Flying Geese units
- 8 – 2½" half-square triangle units
- 4 – 2½" Side A triangles OR triangles from 5¼" square cut 2x diagonally
- 4 – 4½" Side B triangles OR 4 – 4⅞" triangles

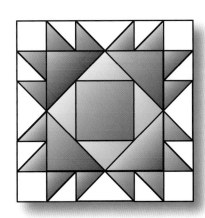

Block # 130
- 6 – 2½" squares
- 2 – 2½" x 10½" rectangles
- 14 – 2½" half-square triangle units
- 3 – 2½" Side B triangles OR 3 – 2⅞" triangles
- 2 – 3" Side A triangles OR triangles from 6¼" square cut 2 x diagonally
- 1 – 1½" x 4¾" rectangle

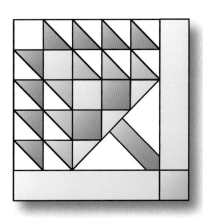

Block # 131
- 4 – 2½″ squares
- 4 – 2½″ x 4½″ Flying Geese units
- 12 – 2½″ half-square triangle units
- 8 – 2½″ triangles
- 1 – 4½″ quad-triangle unit

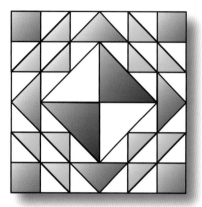

Block # 132
- 8 – 2½″ squares
- 8 – 2½″ x 4½″ Flying Geese units
- 8 – 2½″ half-square triangle units
- 1 – 4½″ square

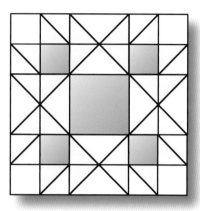

Block # 133
- 2 – 4½″ squares
- 20 – 2½″ squares
- 4 – 2½″ x 4½″ rectangles

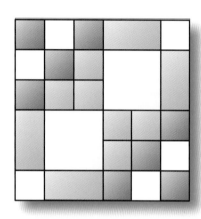

Block # 134
- 1 – 4½″ square
- 8 – 2½″ x 4½″ Flying Geese units
- 16 – 2½″ half-square triangle units

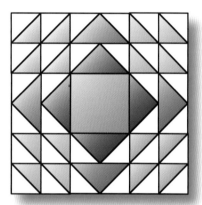

Block # 135
- 8 – 2½″ squares
- 1 – 4½″ square-in-a-square unit
- 4 – 2½″ x 4½″ Flying Geese units
- 8 – 2½″ half-square triangle units
- 8 – 2½″ triple-triangle units

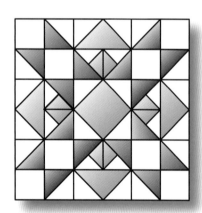

Block # 136
- 8 – 2½″ squares
- 28 – 2½″ half-square triangle units

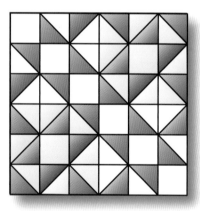

Block # 137
- 1 – 4½″ square
- 8 – 2½″ squares
- 4 – 2½″ x 4½″ rectangles
- 4 – 2½″ x 8½″ rectangles

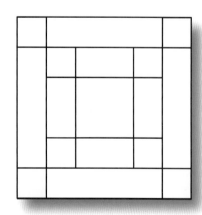

Block # 138
- 18 – 2½″ x 4½″ Flying Geese units

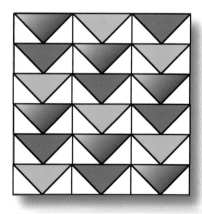

Block # 139
- 5 – 4½" four-patch units
- 4 – 4½" half-square triangle units

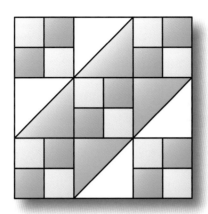

Block # 140
- 12 – 2½" x 6½" rectangles

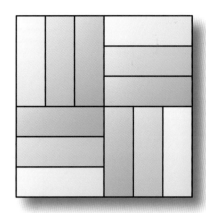

Block # 141
- 1 – 4½" square
- 4 – 4½" half-square triangle units
- 8 – 2½" x 4½" Flying Geese units

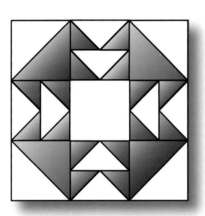

Block # 142
- 8 – 2½" squares
- 4 – 2½" x 6½" rectangles
- 16 – 2½" half-square triangle units

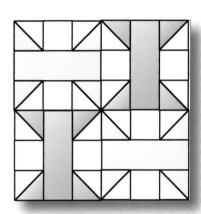

Block # 143
- 9 – 4½" double-rectangle units

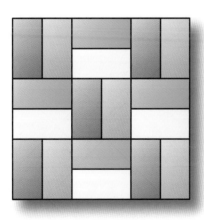

Block # 144
- 4 – 2½" squares
- 4 – 4½" half-square triangle units
- 16 – 2½" half-square triangle units

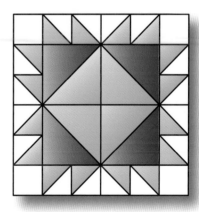

Block # 145
- 1 – 4½" square
- 4 – 2½" squares
- 4 – 2½" x 4½" rectangles
- 4 – 2½" x 4½" Flying Geese units
- 12 – 2½" half-square triangle units

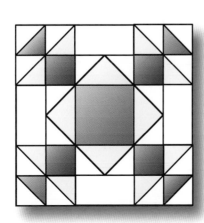

Block # 146
- 4 – 2½" squares
- 1 – 4½" square
- 4 – 4½" double-rectangle units
- 12 – 2½" half-square triangle units

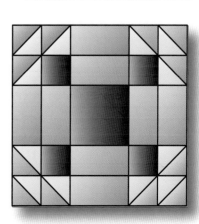

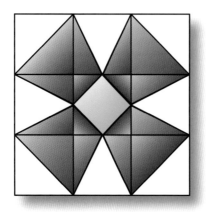

Block # 147

- 1 – 4½" square-in-a-square unit
- 4 – 4½" TRI RECS units
- 4 – 4½" half-square triangle units

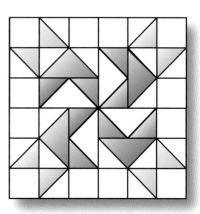

Block # 148

- 12 – 2½" squares
- 8 – 2½" half-square triangle units
- 8 – 2½" x 4½" Flying Geese units

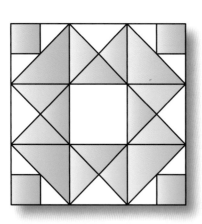

Block # 149

- 1 – 4½" square
- 4 – 4½" quad-triangle units
- 4 – 4½" triangles-square units

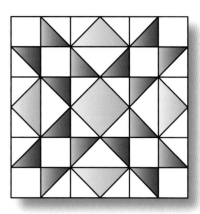

Block # 150

- 8 – 2½" squares
- 8 – 2½" x 4½" Flying Geese units
- 1 – 4½" square-in-a-square unit
- 8 – 2½" half-square triangle units

THE 14" BLOCK GALLERY
(Block size: 14½" unfinished)

Block # 151
- 4 – 4½" x 6½" rectangles
- 4 – 4½" four-patch units
- 1 – 6½" nine-patch unit

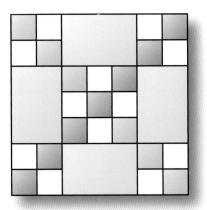

Block # 152
- 5 – 2½" squares
- 4 – 4½" squares
- 4 – 2½" x 6½" rectangles
- 16 – 2½" half-square triangle units

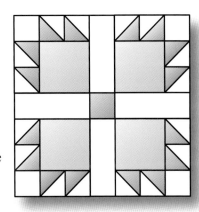

Block # 153
- 12 – 2½" x 4½" Flying Geese units
- 8 – 5¼" triangles
- 8 – 2½" Side A triangles OR 8 – 3⅝" triangles

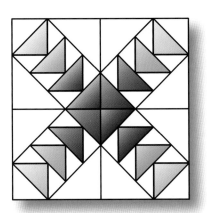

Block # 154
- 5 – 2½" squares
- 4 – 4½" half-square triangle units
- 4 – 2½" x 6½" rectangles
- 16 – 2½" half-square triangle units

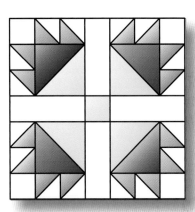

Block # 155
- 5 – 2½" squares
- 4 – 4½" squares
- 4 – 2½" x 6½" rectangles
- 16 – 2½" half-square triangle units

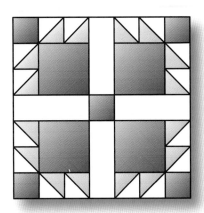

Block # 156
- 1 – 2½" square
- 4 – 4½" squares
- 4 – 2½" x 6½" rectangles
- 20 – 2½" half-square triangle units

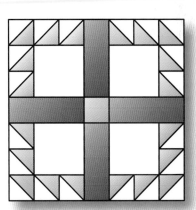

Block # 157
- 17 – 2½" squares
- 4 – 2½" x 6½" rectangles
- 4 – 2½" stem units
- 16 – 2½" half-square triangle units

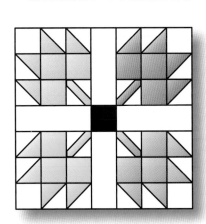

Block # 158
- 5 – 2½" squares
- 4 – 4½" four-patch units
- 4 – 2½" x 6½" rectangles
- 16 – 2½" half-square triangle units

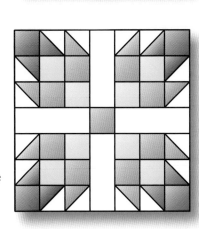

Block # 159

- 25 – 2½" squares
- 4 – 4½" half-square triangle units
- 4 – 2½" x 4½" rectangles

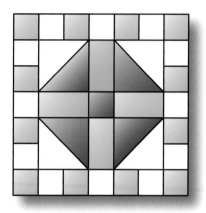

Block # 160

- 21 – 2½" squares
- 16 – 2½" half-square triangle units
- 4 – 2½" x 6½" rectangles

Block # 161

- 5 – 2½" squares
- 4 – 2½" x 6½" rectangles
- 4 – 4½" four-patch units
- 16 – 2½" half-square triangle units

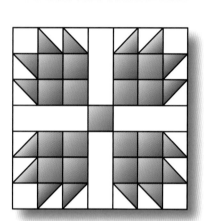

Block # 162

- 12 – 2½" squares
- 16 – 2½" half-square triangle units
- 4 – 2½" x 6½" rectangles
- 1 – 6½" nine-patch unit

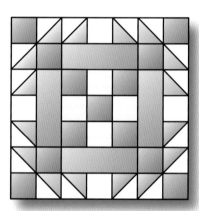

Block # 163

- 5 – 2½" squares
- 4 – 4½" half-square triangle units
- 4 – 2½" x 4½" rectangles
- 20 – 2½" half-square triangle units

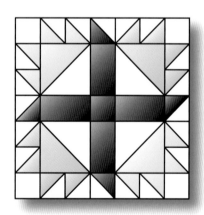

Block # 164

- 13 – 2½" squares
- 4 – 4½" half-square triangle units
- 20 – 2½" half-square triangle units

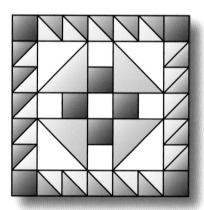

Block # 165

- 17 – 2½" squares
- 4 – 2½" x 6½" rectangles
- 16 – 2½" half-square triangle units
- 4 – 2½" stem units

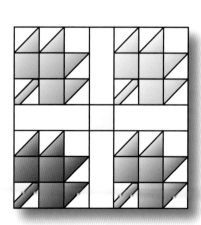

Block # 166

- 1 – 2½" square
- 4 – 4½" squares
- 4 – 2½" x 6½" rectangles
- 20 – 2½" half-square triangle units

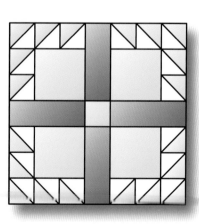

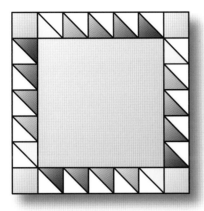

Block # 167
- 1 – 10½" square
- 4 – 2½" squares
- 20 – 2½" half-square triangle units

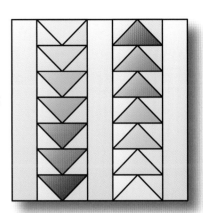

Block # 168
- 14 – 2½" x 4½" Flying Geese units
- 3 – 2½" x 14½" rectangles

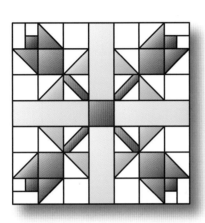

Block # 169
- 4 – 2½" rectangle-squares units
- 13 – 2½" squares
- 16 – 2½" half-square triangle units
- 4 – 2½" stem units
- 4 – 2½" x 6½" rectangles

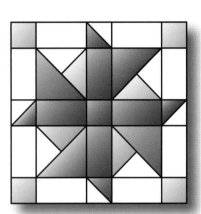

Block # 170
- 5 – 2½" squares
- 12 – 2½" x 4½" rectangles
- 4 – 4½" triple-triangle units
- 4 – 2½" half-square triangle units

TRY THIS!

One of my favorite things to do when I buy a new quilt book is to take it to my local office supply store and have them cut off the spine and replace it with a spiral binding. This costs just a few dollars and takes only a few minutes but it is oh, so worth it! Your book will lie flat on your cutting table or next to your machine as you sew so you don't have to worry about losing your place on the page!

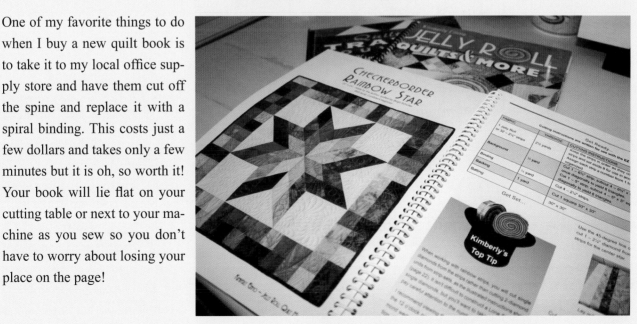

THE 16" BLOCK GALLERY
(Block size: 16½" unfinished)

Block # 171
- 4 – 2½" squares
- 5 – 4½" four-patch units
- 4 – 2½" x 4½" rectangles
- 4 – 4½" x 6½" rectangles

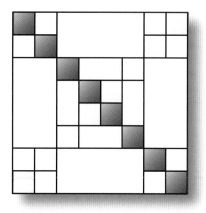

Block # 172
- 1 – 4½" square

12 rectangles:
- 1 – 2½" x 4½"
- 2 – 2½" x 6½"
- 2 – 2½" x 8½"
- 2 – 2½" x 10½"
- 2 – 2½" x 12½"
- 2 – 2½" x 14½"
- 1 – 2½" x 16½"

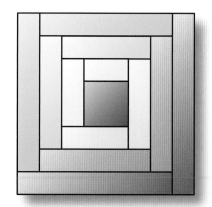

Block # 173
- 16 – 2½" x 8½" rectangles

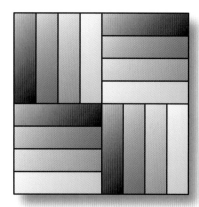

Block # 174
- 8 – 4½" half-square triangle units
- 8 – 4½" double-rectangle units

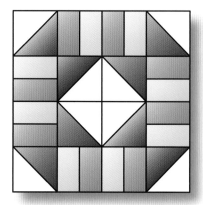

Block # 175
- 4 – 4½" squares
- 16 – 2½" squares
- 16 – 2½" x 4½" Flying Geese units

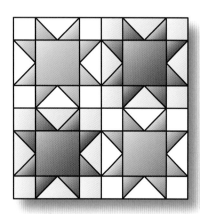

Block # 176
- 4 – 2½" squares
- 1 – 4½" square
- 4 – 4½" four-patch units
- 8 – 2½" x 4½" rectangles
- 4 – 4½" x 6½" rectangles

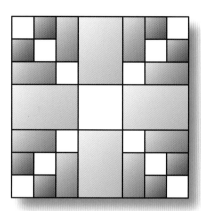

Block # 177
- 40 – 2½" half-square triangle units
- 16 – 2½" triangles
- 8 – 4½" triangles

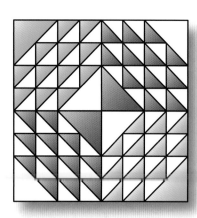

Block # 178
- 4 – 4½" four-patch units
- 4 – 4½" x 8½" double-rectangle units
- 2 – 4½" squares
- 2 – 4½" half-square triangle units

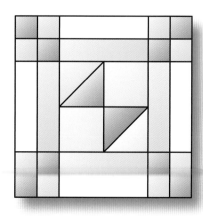

Block # 179

- 5 – 4½" four-patch units
- 4 – 4½" squares
- 12 – 2½" squares
- 8 – 2½" x 4½" rectangles

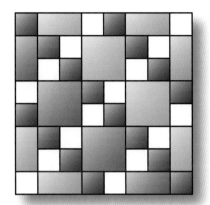

Block # 180

- 3 – 4½" x 16½" rectangles
- 16 – 2½" half-square triangle units

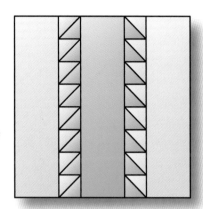

Block # 181

- 1 – 4½" square
- 4 – 2½" squares
- 4 – 2½" x 4½" Flying Geese units
- 4 – 4½" x 8½" Flying Geese units
- 4 – 4½" half-square triangle units

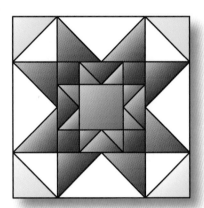

Block # 182

- 1 – 4½" square
- 4 – 4½" four-patch units
- 4 – 4½" double-rectangle units
- 8 – 2½" x 4½" rectangles
- 4 – 2½" squares
- 4 – 2½" x 4½" Flying Geese units

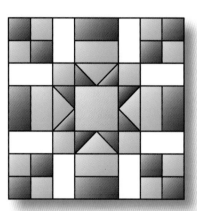

Block # 183

- 1 – 8½" square
- 4 – 6½" triangles
- 4 – 4½" triangles
- 20 – 2½" half-square triangle units
- 8 – 2½" Side B triangles OR 8 – 2⅞" triangles

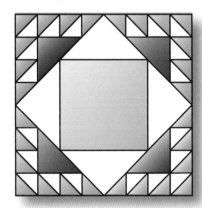

Block # 184

- 1 – 8½" square
- 8 – 2½" squares
- 8 – 2½" half-square triangle units
- 8 – 2½" Side B triangles OR 8 – 2⅞" triangles
- 4 – 2½" x 4½" Flying Geese units
- 4 – 2½" Side A triangles OR 4 – 2⅞" triangles

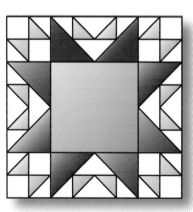

Block # 185

- 1 – 4½" square
- 4 – 6½" nine-patch units
- 4 – 4½" x 6½" triple-rectangle units

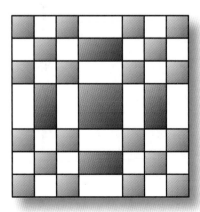

Block # 186

- 1 – 4½" square
- 4 – 4½" x 6½" rectangles
- 4 – 4½" four-patch units
- 4 – 2½" squares
- 16 – 2½" half-square triangle units

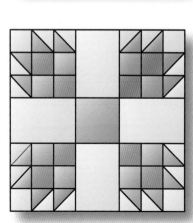

Block # 187

- 5 – 4½" squares
- 4 – 4½" x 8½" Flying Geese units
- 4 – 2½" squares
- 4 – 2½" x 4½" Flying Geese units

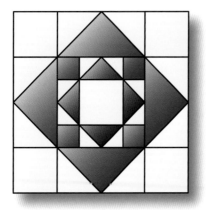

Block # 188

1 – 4½" square
12 – 2½" squares
8 – 2½" half-square triangle units
8 – 4½" triangles
8 – 2½" x 4½" Flying Geese units
4 – 2½" Side A triangles

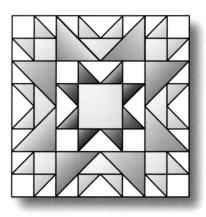

Block # 189

- 20 – 2½" squares
- 44 – 2½" half-square triangle units

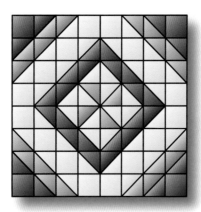

Block # 190

- 1 – 8½" square
- 4 – 4½" squares
- 16 – 2½" x 4½" Flying Geese units

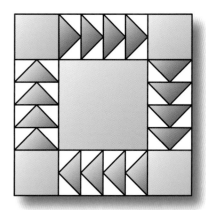

Block # 191

- 5 – 4½" squares
- 4 – 4½" x 6½" rectangles
- 4 – 2½" squares
- 16 – 2½" half-square triangle units

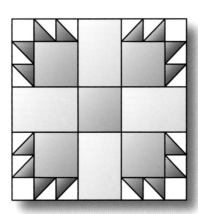

Block # 192

- 12 – 2½" squares
- 5 – 4½" four-patch units
- 16 – 2½" x 4½" Flying Geese units

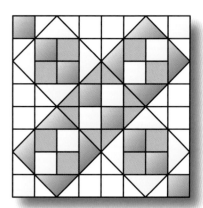

BIG BLOCKS – Perfect for working with Charm Packs or Layer Cakes. Blocks can be sized as 16", 20", or 24".

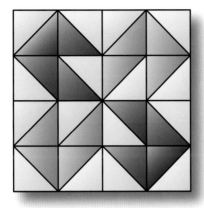

Block # 193
- 16 half-square triangle units

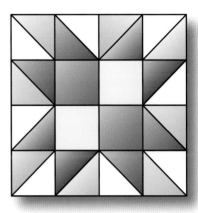

Block # 194
- 1 four-patch unit
- 12 half-square triangle units

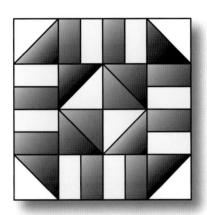

Block # 195
- 8 half-square triangle units
- 8 double-rectangle units

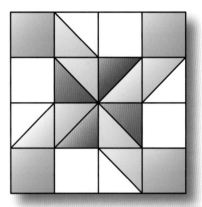

Block # 196
- 8 squares
- 8 half-square triangle units

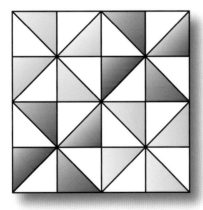

Block # 197
- 16 half-square triangle units

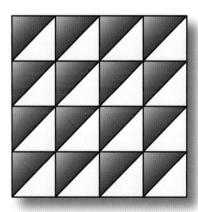

Block # 198
- 16 half-square triangle units

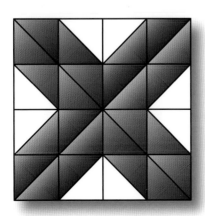

Block # 199
- 16 half-square triangle units

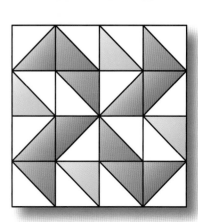

Block # 200
- 16 half-square triangle units

EXPAND YOUR DESIGN OPPORTUNITIES

Think about the grid.

Now that you've mastered the basics of block building, I'd like to show you how to expand your design horizons and embrace your inner creative diva (and I know there's one inside you just waiting to come out!). There are many exciting yet easy things you can do to create beautiful quilts from precuts which will be as unique as you are. To begin, consider blocks as grids because actually, that's all they are when you break them down. Most pieced blocks, such as those featured in the block library, will fall within two basic categories: Nine-Patch and Four-Patch blocks. Typically block sizes that are easily divisible by 3 (6", 9", 12", 15", and so on) make easy Nine-Patch blocks. Block sizes that are easily divisible by 2 (8", 12", 16", 20" and so on) make easy Four-Patch blocks. Teach yourself to look at any pieced block and visualize how it might break down as a grid.

For example, the blocks below are basic Nine-Patch blocks made up of nine equal sections:

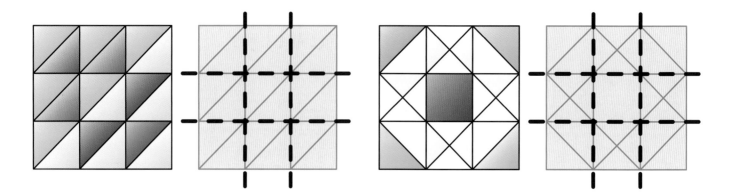

The blocks below are basic Four-Patch blocks, made up of four equal quadrants.

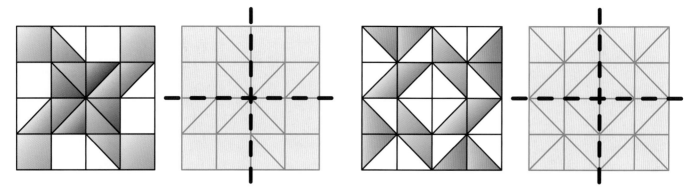

Think about variation inside the grid.

You've heard the old expression, "There's more than one way to skin a cat." Well, sometimes there is more than one way to piece a block! Once you learn to look at each block and break it down into manageable sections in your mind (or on graph paper, if necessary), you can decide how you want to cut and stitch the units to piece your block together. Consider the following example:

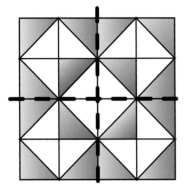

The block shown breaks down into a basic Four-Patch block. Without the patches defined by black lines (or seam lines) it can be confusing to visualize how the block units are pieced. However, there are several different ways to piece this block! Take a look.

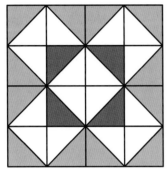

This version has been divided into 16 half-square triangle units.

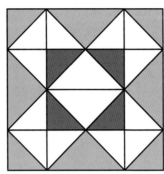

This version has been divided into 6 Flying Geese units and 4 half-square triangle units.

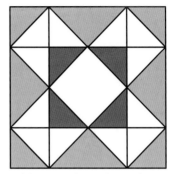

This version has been divided into 1 square-in-a-square unit, 4 half-square triangle units, and 4 Flying Geese units.

In this example, the block breaks down into a basic Four-Patch. Without the black lines to define each patch, try to visualize which units might be sewn. There are several options for pieced units that will work.

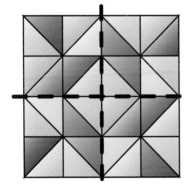

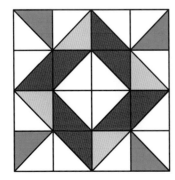

This version has been divided into 16 half-square triangle units. Notice that it has the same components as the first example above, yet has an entirely different look.

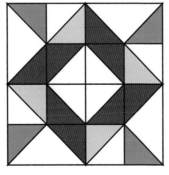

This version has been divided into 4 Flying Geese units and 8 half-square triangle units.

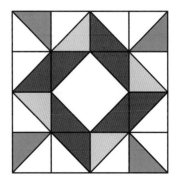

This version has been divided into 1 square-in-a-square and 12 half-square triangle units.

Think inside the block.

The center of some blocks makes the perfect canvas for adding interesting design elements, which will ultimately create a new and interesting block. Consider one of my personal favorite blocks, the Sawtooth Star. If you look at the center square, it can easily be converted into a basic four-patch unit. But oh, my goodness, there are so many things you can do with that design space! Consider adding simple basic units inside the star's center square to create a new design as illustrated below:

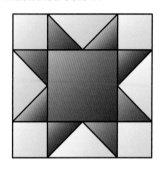
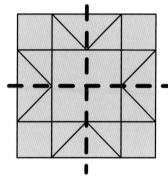

Do you see the "invisible" four-patch units created in the center? In an 8" finished block, that four-patch unit would be made up of four 2½" unfinished squares. In a 16" finished block, the four-patch unit would be made up of four – 4½" unfinished squares.

Let's take the same basic Sawtooth Star block and consider just a few of the design options simply by adding different four-patch units in the center. The center of the star really is a design canvas where you can showcase a wide variety of interesting and unique elements. Be creative!

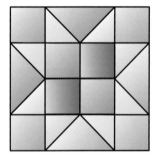
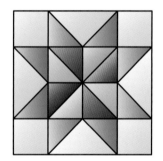
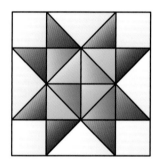
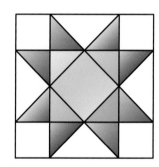

Think value.

Fabrics and color are certainly important factors to consider when piecing your blocks. But value may be one of the most important factors to consider as it will certainly increase the number of design options you have. Value is defined as the relative lightness or darkness of a color. *Where you place the values within a block determines how the block will look.*

Consider the example below and a few of the many different ways the block might look depending on where the values are placed within the same layout. This is a basic Four-Patch block composed of eight Flying Geese units. However, the layout is transformed when the light, medium, and dark value placements are changed within the units.

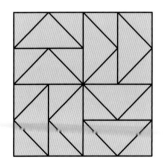
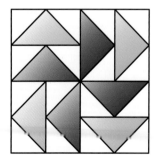
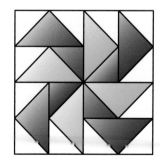
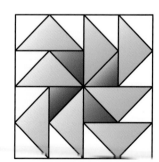

Use pencil to draw your blocks on graph paper or use your computer design software (I love using Electric Quilt software) to test the value placement within your blocks before you actually cut your fabrics and begin to sew. You'll be amazed at how differently the same block can look depending on where you place the light, medium, and dark value fabrics! Test a variety of options to see which you like best. The possibilities are endless!

Think scale.

The next design element to consider is the scale of your fabrics. In most cases when you use a purchased bundle of strips or precuts, there is typically a wide range of scale of prints, which will create a dynamic quilt. Personally I think quilts are the most interesting visually and have the most "sparkle" or panache when there is a varied range of scale of fabrics used to construct the blocks. And by all means, don't shy away from using large-scale prints— even in small-size blocks. You may have to "fussy cut" to avoid blank background areas when working with large-scale prints, but it is well worth the effort.

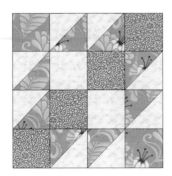 

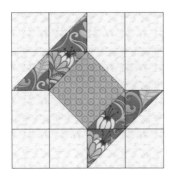 

Think stripes and geometrics.

How many times have you heard from an instructor or read in a book or pattern to avoid using directional or geometric prints? Too many times to count, but I say au contraire. Use them! Stripes and plaids don't have to match (seriously!) and in fact when they don't match, they add movement, excitement, texture, and a special verve and zippiness to your quilts. Use directional prints or stripes and don't worry in which direction they'll end up in your blocks. Throw caution to the wind and let go of your old inhibitions. Be bold, step out of your comfort zone, and use those striped and directional beauties. (And if anyone questions your decision to do so, tell them proudly that I gave you permission and said it was okay!)

KIMBERLY'S TOP TIP

In most cases, when using purchased precut fabric bundles, you'll find a good assortment of values—plenty of lights, mediums, and darks. But once in a while, you might run across a bundle with fabrics that are mostly medium in value. What to do? First of all, don't panic! You have options. I think the best thing to do is plan to use this group of medium-value fabrics with one light (or one very dark) non-busy background fabric. I prefer to use solid fabrics, tone-on-tone prints, or mottled fabrics that "read" like a solid. Don't use a background fabric that is busy; it will only fight with your medium fabrics and your quilt will end up looking chaotic. By using a very light solid-ish fabric as your background, you'll create negative spaces in your quilt where the viewer's eye can rest. This helps calm the chaos and provide the necessary definition in your blocks for your design to really have an impact and look balanced.

Think outside the box.

Once you have decided which blocks to use to create your quilt, the next step is to decide how you want to set them together. Don't be daunted by choices and decisions. Just take the process one step at a time.

There is an almost unlimited number of settings you can use. Below are just a few of the possible options—a sampling of the most common and easy-to-use.

For even more ideas, peruse quilt books and magazines or search the Internet. Study the block settings of quilts that appeal to you. Most importantly, don't stress over this decision. Consider the various possibilities by laying out your blocks and auditioning fabrics for sashing and borders. Have fun choosing the layout you like best.

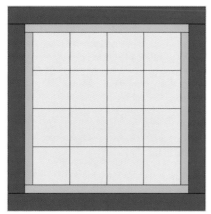

Straight-set blocks

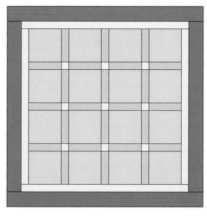

Straight-set blocks with sashing and cornerstones

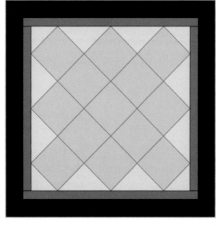

Blocks set on point with setting triangles

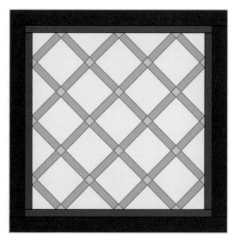

Blocks set on point with sashing, cornerstones, and setting triangles

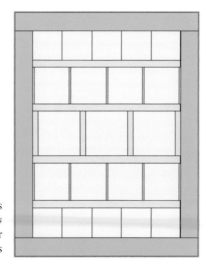

Horizontal rows of blocks with varied block sizes with sashing and spacer strips

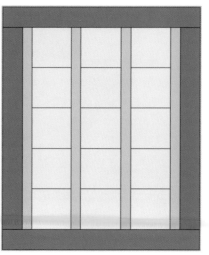

Vertical rows of blocks with vertical sashing strips

Think alternate setting blocks.

Don't overlook a simple yet fantastic design opportunity! There are dozens of blocks in the block library you can use to create a simple alternate block setting that will create a dynamic layout with stunning secondary designs.

In the examples here, the blank squares are where you would add your pieced blocks. Let your mind run wild with the amazing possiblilities. For a jump start, consider these alternate block settings. Test a variety of blocks as alternate setting blocks. You will be surprised at the different effects you can achieve.

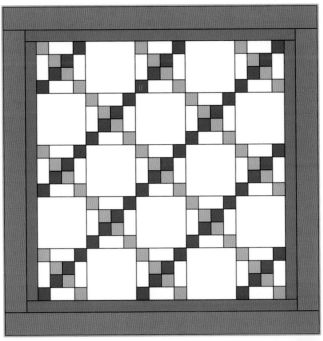

Chain blocks are a classic way to add the illusion of a diagonal set to straight-set blocks.

Use four-patch and half-square triangle units (here in Jacob's Ladder blocks) to create an interesting secondary design for your blocks.

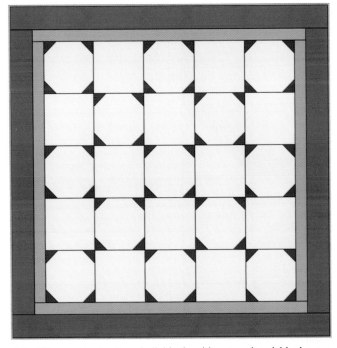

Alternating a simple Snowball block with your pieced blocks can create an interesting effect.

Here's another block that will create a diagonal feel to your setting.

Test a variety of blocks as alternate setting blocks. You will be surprised at the different effects you can achieve.

Think BIG BLOCK Palooza!

Yes, when it comes to blocks, size does matter. Your design options expand even more when you begin to consider enlarging standard-size blocks into BIG sizes—16", 20", and even 24". Big blocks are fun, easy to make, and allow you to make the best use of 10" squares and fat quarters while constructing large quilts in a jiffy.

Just like those golden arches value meals, almost any block can be super-sized with just a few quick calculations. It all goes back to viewing each block as a grid. Consider blocks #193 – #200 (page 51). These are just a few of the many that are easy to up-size.

This 8" block breaks down into 4 four-patch units, as shown by the dashed red lines. Each smaller unit within the four-patch unit measures 2½" unfinished, as shown by the blue dashed lines. If you resize each 2½" square unit to a 4½" (unfinished) square, the block will become a 16" Big Block.

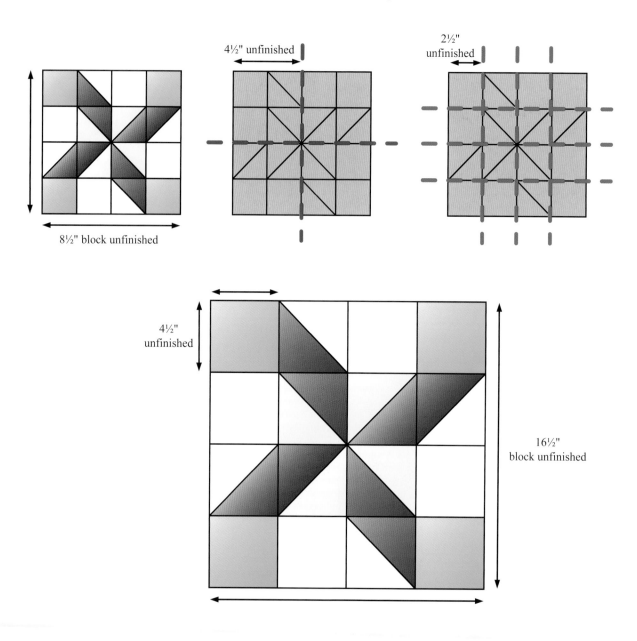

8½" block unfinished

4½" unfinished

2½" unfinished

4½" unfinished

16½" block unfinished

SIMPLY STUNNING SAMPLERS

In recent years, sampler quilts have experienced a vigorous comeback, which I think is a refreshing change from the rather boring reputation they earned in the past couple of decades. In some quilting circles, sampler quilts were considered old-fashioned or dare I say "stodgy." I used to hear comments that sampler quilts were the types of quilts made by pioneer women or somebody's grandmother and were therefore outdated. Still others thought sampler quilts were just a utilitarian use for orphan blocks or the result of winning a guild's monthly block raffle. Pretty? Yes. But as a design dynamo? Maybe not so much. Quite honestly, I think even now some quilters think samplers are a big snooze-fest!

But I say, *NO MORE*. Sampler quilts have made a triumphant comeback and with today's fabrics and modern design sense, samplers can be bold, dynamic, a visual feast for the eyes, and a great way to build precision piecing skills. How's that for a one-two punch?

Not only are sampler quilts a fantastic way to perfect your piecing skills but making these blocks from your pile of coordinated strips is just plain F-U-N. If you only have five, fifteen, or twenty-five minutes to sew, you can actually accomplish a lot in that short amount of time and you'll be amazed at just how much mileage you can get from those strips. Sampler quilts are true classics, always fashionable, and a wonderful way to discover which blocks you enjoy piecing the most. I want to encourage you to create your own simply stunning sampler quilt. In the process, you'll create a gorgeous heirloom—one that will be cherished in years to come by your ancestors who will praise you for being fashion-forward and trendy!

LONESTAR SAMPLER
48" x 48", made by the author
Quilted by Birgit Schüller
Medallion center block size: 20"
Sampler block size: 6"
Skill level: Intermediate

GET READY...

Cutting instructions are written for use with EZ Flying Geese Ruler, EZ Jelly Roll Ruler, and the TRI RECS Tools.

FABRIC	YARDAGE	INSTRUCTIONS
1 Jelly Roll or 40 – 2½" strips	2½ yards	• Choose two medium matching (or closely matching) strips and set aside for "radiant" middle ring of center Lonestar. • Select 2 additional contrasting strips for the center and outer star points of Lonestar. • Use the remaining strips to construct the blocks.
Background Fabric	1¾ yards	• Cut 1 – 6⅝" strip; subcut 4 – 6⅝" squares and cut each square once diagonally to yield 8 triangles. • Cut 1 – 5" strip; subcut 4 – 5" squares and cut each square once diagonally to yield 8 triangles. • Use the remaining yardage to construct the blocks.
First Inner Border and Binding	¾ yard	• Use 2 Jelly Roll strips cut in half lengthwise to create 4 – 1¼" x 40" strips OR cut 4 – 1¼" strips.
Second Inner Border	½ yard	Cut 4 – 2½" strips.
Outer Border	1½ yards	Cut 4 – 5½" strips from 54" length of fabric.
Backing	3 yards	2 panels 28" x 56"
Batting		56" x 56"

GET SET...

KIMBERLY'S TOP TIP

Challenge yourself to use at least a little bit of fabric from every Jelly Roll strip to construct your sampler blocks. You may want to fussy-cut some of the strips to make the best use of medium- or large-scale prints. The more fabrics you incorporate, the more your quilt will sparkle with excitement. However, I recommend that you use a solid fabric or a mottled fabric that "reads" like a solid for the background. It is very important for you to give the viewer's eyes a place to rest.

SEW

- Follow the instructions on pages 18–21 to piece the center Lonestar block.
- Add 1¼" strips around the center medallion block.
- Piece your choice of 16 – 6" (finished) blocks to add around the medallion block.
- Use 1½" x 6½" spacing strips of background fabric between your sampler blocks. You may need to adjust the width of these strips to make the borders fit around the center block.
- Add additional borders as desired.
- Don't forget rickrack, trims, etc.—the possibilities for embellishment are endless.
- Baste, quilt, bind, and enjoy!

Thoughts about the quilting from Birgit

Because the fabrics used to create this quilt were whimsical, the quilt called for some cheerful quilting designs. Each diamond is quilted with a swirly design in the middle that allows the machine to travel conveniently from diamond to diamond, and therefore from one star section to the next. To keep the designs cohesive and to continue the same theme, variations of those swirly designs can be found in other areas of the quilt and in each of the different sampler blocks. The background areas of the blocks were quilted simply with a stipple fill. The inner and middle striped borders are quilted with tight roping in the narrow areas and Greek spirals in the wider border. These elements kept the whimsical and cheerful feeling. Since the outer border featured a very busy print, free-form feathers were the perfect finishing touch to keep the stitching balanced across the surface of the quilt.

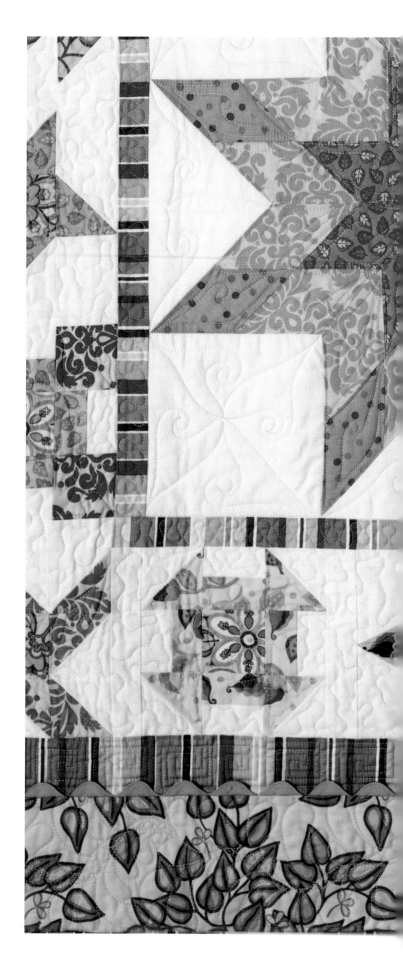

TRY THIS

Use Jumbo Rickrack to create an exciting scalloped edge!

I've discovered a fun and fabulous design and embellishment opportunity—jumbo rickrack! Recently it has become readily available in local quilt and hobby shops and increasingly popular with quilters. Now I know why!

As I laid out the outer border for my 6" sampler quilt, I thought to myself that while it looked pretty, it lacked a certain sparkle. Then, while wandering around my local quilt shop one day, I noticed bright aqua rickrack on a large spool winking at me from across the room. It was just the perfect shade of aqua and I knew it would add the right "zing" to my otherwise lovely-but-rather-sedate quilt.

I used my favorite appliqué glue to secure the rickrack before adding my outer border. Once the border was stitched in place, I trimmed the excess "points" from the opposite side to reduce bulk in the seams. It was like adding perfect little curved Prairie Points without the bother of having to make them. Try this quick, easy, fun, and convenient option.

ON-POINT SAMPLER

41" x 41", made by the author
Quilted by Birgit Schüller
Block size: 8"
Skill level: Intermediate

GET READY...

Cutting instructions are written for use with EZ Flying Geese Ruler, EZ Jelly Roll Ruler, and the TRI RECS Tools.

FABRIC	YARDAGE	INSTRUCTIONS
1 Jelly Roll or 40 – 2½" strips	2½ yards	• Divide strips into piles of lights, mediums, and darks. • Use the strips to piece your choice of 8" blocks.
Background Fabric	2 yards	• Cut 2 – 4½" strips; subcut 32 – 2½" x 4½" rectangles for the Chain blocks. • Cut 4 – 8½" strips; subcut 64 – 2½" x 8½" rectangles for sashing strips. • Use the remaining fabric to piece 8" blocks.
Fabric #1 (Aqua)	¾ yard	• Cut 1 – 9¼" strip; subcut 4 – 9¼" x 9¼" squares. Cut each square twice diagonally to yield 16 setting triangles. • Cut 3 – 2½" strips; subcut 48 – 2½" x 2½" squares. Set aside 32 squares for the Chain blocks and 16 squares for cornerstones.
Fabric #2 (Red) includes binding	1 yard	• Cut 3 – 2½" strips; subcut 40 – 2½" x 2½" squares for the Chain blocks. • From remaining 2½" strip (above), cut 2 – 1⅞" x 1⅞" squares. Cut each square once diagonally to yield 4 corner triangles. • Cut 1 – 3¼" strip; subcut 3 – 3¼" x 3¼" squares. Cut each square twice diagonally to yield 12 small setting triangles. • Cut 5 – 2¼" strips for the binding.
Backing	2⅞ yards	• 2 panels 24" x 49"
Batting		• 49" x 49"

GET SET...

KIMBERLY'S TOP TIP

The reason this particular on-point setting is so striking is because the Chain blocks draw the eye inward and tie the blocks together for a truly planned and cohesive look. The four Star blocks in the center are similar yet different; this also contributes to making the overall design work so well. This quilt is another way to perfect your piecing skills and try out a few new 8" blocks. Although this quilt looks difficult to piece, you'll discover how easy it is to assemble by sewing the blocks and setting triangles together in rows! Begin by constructing the Chain blocks. Then, choose four blocks for the center of the quilt. From there, let the fabrics and block options "speak" to you and decide as you go. You'll enjoy a new sense of freedom as you create a quilt "from scratch" that will look as if you planned every last detail with incredible care! The secret? Let the blocks and coordinated fabrics do the work for you!

SEW!

- Use 16 – 2½" x 2½" squares each of Fabric #1 and #2 to make 8 Four-Patch blocks.
- Press seams toward darker fabric.
- Blocks should measure 4½" unfinished. Square up if necessary.

Make 8

- Sew 2 – 2½" x 4½" background fabric rectangles to each side of all 8 four-patch units.
- Press the seams toward the background fabric rectangles.

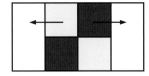

- Sew a 2½" Fabric #1 square and 2½" Fabric #2 square to each side of a 2½" x 4½" background fabric rectangle.
- Make 16 units. Press seams towards the background fabric rectangles.

- Add rectangle units to four-patch units to make the Chain blocks.
- Press seams away from the four-patch units.
- Blocks should measure 8½" square unfinished. Make 8 Chain blocks.

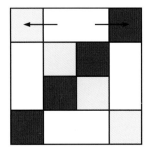

- Piece your choice of 16 – 8" blocks, 4 for the center medallion and 12 to add around the center.
- Use 2½" x 8½" sashing strips and 2½" x 2½" corner-stones to create the on-point setting.
- Add setting triangles to each row and assemble row by row. You may need to adjust the width of these strips to make the borders fit around the center blocks.

- Add additional borders if desired, or finish the quilt as shown.
- Baste, quilt, bind, and enjoy!

Thoughts about the quilting from Birgit

I have found I need to approach a sampler quilt top differently from one where the same blocks are used over and over again. The biggest issue to consider with this particular sampler quilt is that all the background areas around the various blocks are different! What to do? Since there were no defined sections in this quilt, I decided to create them! Circles seemed to be a good choice.

The next problem was what would I use when I didn't have a 10½" circle guide amongst my numerous quilting notions? My approach involved a trip to my kitchen cabinet and finding the right size dinner plate amongst my tableware to assist in my quilting endeavor. Good thing that my size estimation capability didn't fail me. My dinner plate was assigned a new purpose as quilting guide!

At first, I quilted my large circles around the pieced blocks. Stepping back, I realized that semicircles towards the border and additional full circles around the Four-Patch blocks would complement the impression of interlinked rings! After I had defined the spaces, I stitched-in-the-ditch around the pieced blocks and kept the quilting rather simple using mainly swirly designs and continuous curves.

I decided to leave the melon-shaped arcs created by the overlapping circles unquilted. In order to make them pop, I needed a small-scale background filler. Since Kimberly had asked me to avoid stippling if at all possible, I ran wild with pebbles! As I had wanted to give curved crosshatching a try for quite a while, the setting triangles were my field of dreams! Encouraged by the faux trapunto effect of the unquilted areas in the quilt's center portion, I opted to take up this effect in my border quilting where I continued every other curved crosshatching line and filled the background sections with more pebbles. I am so pleased with the overall effect of the quilting and the quilt!

RAINBOW GONE WILD!

49" x 49", made by the author

Quilted by Birgit Schüller
Block size: 6"
Skill level: Skilled Intermediate
(but so worth the effort!)

GET READY...

Cutting instructions are written for use with EZ Flying Geese Ruler, EZ Jelly Roll Ruler, and the TRI RECS Tools.

FABRIC	YARDS	INSTRUCTIONS
1 Rainbow Jelly Roll or 40 – 2½" strips	2½ yards	• Begin by sorting your strips into 8 distinct color groups to piece the blocks—yellows, oranges, reds, pinks, aqua, blues, greens, and purples. • You may have to adjust the color groups based on the number of colors you have in your fabric strips . • Cut pieces from strips as needed to construct your sampler blocks. Follow color placement in chart below. • Cut 41 – 2½" squares from a variety of colors for the cornerstones.
Background Fabric	4½ yards	• Cut pieces as needed to construct your sampler blocks. • Cut 2 – 2¼" squares; cut once diagonally to yield 4 corner setting sashing triangles. • Cut 4 – 4⅛" squares; cut twice diagonally to yield 16 side setting sashing triangles. • Cut 5 – 9¾" squares; cut twice diagonally to yield 20 side setting triangles. • Cut 100 – 2½" x 6½" sashing pieces. • Cut 5 – 3½" strips; piece as necessary for the outer borders. • Cut 6 – 2¼" strips; piece for the binding.
Backing	4¼ yards	• 2 panels 36" x 68"
Batting		• 68" x 68"

GET SET...

KIMBERLY'S TOP TIP

This quilt will look stunning whether you use a white, light, or a dark background as I did. Of course you don't have to use rainbow-colored strips to piece your blocks; any precut strip bundle will look equally as pretty, or you could also choose a wide variety of scrappy fabrics. No matter which color option you select, I suggest keeping the background fabric as a solid or a tone-on-tone print that "reads" like a solid. The blocks themselves are very busy and the quilt could easily become overwhelmingly chaotic without the calming effect of a solid-looking background. If you don't want to use a solid fabric, consider using a mottled or marble fabric that adds visual interest but still provides that calming effect and lets the pieced blocks be the real stars of this quilt! If you want more definition between the blocks, use a different fabric for your sashing strips.

6" BLOCK SAMPLER GONE WILD!

- Choose a total of 40 – 6" finished blocks or follow my block pattern as provided in the chart below.
- After your blocks are pieced, lay them out with the sashing, cornerstones, and setting triangles. Join them in diagonal rows.
- Sew the rows together and add the outer borders as desired.
- Baste, quilt, bind, and enjoy!

Layout of 6" blocks with sashing, cornerstones, and setting triangles.

Layout of color groups in horizontal rows.

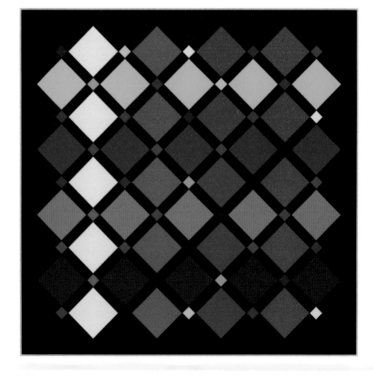

Thoughts about the quilting from Birgit

When I saw this sampler quilt for the first time, I knew right away that it needed some clever quilting to help add a visual structure which would accentuate the underlying concept of the rows. This concept is based on a row-by-row gradation of colors—both vertically and horizontally—creating the impression of a woven grid. All the blocks in a vertical or horizontal row are constructed using colors of the same color family with a solid black background.

Prior to quilting, I realized the problem was that, due to being separated by black sashing strips, the blocks lost their clear-cut definition and seemed to flow into each other. This became my starting point. My goal was to reintroduce some definition to the blocks. As quite often with sampler quilts, I called circles to the rescue! I chose different matching variegated thread colors for the individual color rows of blocks. Using Kim Brunner's Nested Circles templates, I framed each block with a circle. In the sashing strips, these circles overlap slightly which adds more interest. The black backgrounds of the "circular" blocks were filled with tight stippling which made it appear "less black." As I treated all the blocks of one row in the same way using the same color thread, a new accent was given to the individual rows to underline the grid concept—and the desired effect was achieved. Mission accomplished!

Sampler quilts are especially effective if you use rainbow strip rolls. You'll find them in solid, tone-on-tones, mottled, or batik fabrics.

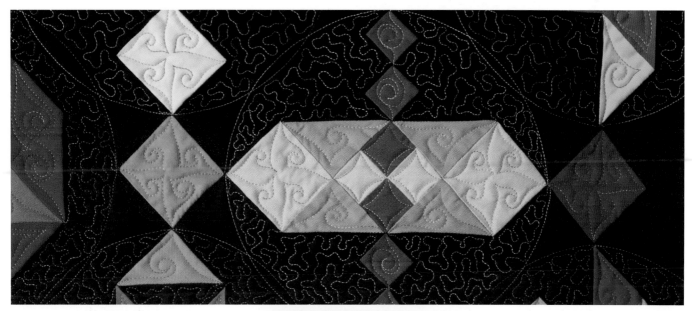

Once I untied the bow, I arranged my fabrics by color group. Then it was easy to use the piles to create the blocks for the rainbow sampler quilt.

Enjoy these fabulous quilts made by combining blocks from the block library to create new, stunning designs!

There is so much you can create with the unlimited design potential of precut bundles or fabrics from your stash and scrap basket. For me personally, writing this book has been a fun and exciting adventure. I combined all my best helpful hints, time and money saving tricks, library of blocks, and design ideas so you can enjoy being your own creative diva to design uniquely individual quilts!

Although I've included tons of ideas in the preceding pages, I'd like to present a small gallery of gorgeous quilts that were designed and made by my international quilting friends. You may have "met" most of them on the pages of my previous books, but if not, please stop by my website at www.kimberlyeinmo.com and allow me to introduce them to you. I hope you'll have hours of inspiration and fun designing your own quilts from precuts and perhaps you'll share a photo with me on my website or on Facebook!

DREAM CATCHER, 58" x 58", made by Claire Neal, UK; quilted by Birgit Schüller

Claire says:

I have been quilting for fifteen years and had never designed my own pattern, so I had no idea where to begin! I had an endless number of beautiful blocks to choose from, beautiful fabrics, and the know-how to piece. So I began with a pencil and graph paper and drew out my favorite blocks. Then I sat back and took the best of those, tried to apply color, and started over! It was rewarding when I found blocks that worked well together—so well that they created a secondary pattern that I chose to highlight by using red to create the diamond effect with red stars.

The blocks were similar but the color placement is what made the secondary pattern emerge. The math and the piecing were the easy part! I loved the fabrics and colors. I had recently been given a dreamcatcher by a close friend to help me with my sleepless nights. This quilt was so therapeutic for me to work on and the many HSTs reminded me of the dreamcatcher, and that became the name of the quilt. This was a really scary first for me, but it turned out to be one of the most rewarding projects I have ever worked on. Give it a try!

SINGING STARS, 50" x 52", made by Christine LaCroix, France

Christine says:

This quilt is a combination of two different blocks – #52 and #181. When I began the design process, I discovered that I could create a larger star by using block #52 four times. I like bright colors, so I chose to use them on the #181 blocks. When I combined the blocks, the bright colors became the focal point of the quilt. I like the way the lighter colored stars help to emphasize the secondary design.

The fabric line I used had a pretty bird print, so I used that in the borders. This helped me come up with a name for my quilt. I wanted to accentuate the stars, so I carefully planned how I would machine quilt the top. I quilted quite heavily in the background and lightly quilted a path around the red fabrics. I simply stitched in the ditch around the stars.

FALLING RIGHT IN PLACE, 47½" x 57", made by Carla Connor, The Netherlands

Carla says:

My thoughts were running wild as I was looking at all the choices I had. My eyes fell on block #35, sometimes called Capital T. I saw a Card Trick block with an interesting pattern in it. So I started playing around and flipping the block around a bit. I liked the pattern that came out of my "playtime" and the variety of fabric colors I could use for this—perfect for using Jelly Rolls and other precut fabrics. It was a breeze making the quilt using Kimberly's EZ Flying Geese Ruler!

**Splash, 62" x 62",
made by Birgit Schüller,
Germany**

Birgit says:

While visiting Kimberly at her home in the summer of 2011, she presented me with a set of Stonehenge Bright Stone Strips by Northcott Fabric plus a 112" cut of cream-colored Stonehenge background fabric. The task was this: I was to pick a few blocks from her block library for this book to design and make a quilt from the fabrics. When I got back home to Germany and spread out the 40 – 2½" wide fabric strips, I noticed some of them were nicely marbled tone-on-tones while others combined several colors from different areas of the color wheel. This did not make it easy to design a suitable quilt top!

I scrolled though Kimberly's block library and ended up selecting blocks #31, #60, and #124. Next I played around a bit with my Electric Quilt software and came up with the design and color placement that I used.

When starting to cut the patches from my fabric strips, I couldn't help but remember our visit to the Artist's Paint Pot geyser in Yellowstone National Park during the summer on that same vacation to the USA. This was exactly how I felt working with these bright and colorful strips—like diving headfirst into a quilter's paint pot with a loud SPLASH! The word stuck in my mind and later became the name of this quilt. Although there were shades of several colors that at first did not seem to go together at all, everything added up to a harmonious entity in the end.

My experience working on this quilt was a thoroughly fascinating process. When the piecing was done, the excitement continued to build with the quilting! I love to play with quilted and unquilted areas and to apply a secondary design in suitable larger background areas. As so many of my quilts, this one also called for an irregular edge treatment, which I think adds a lot of extra interest to the piece.

It's not just the pieced stars that make this quilt shine. Approximately 4,500 Swarovski hot fix crystals were used to really make this quilt sparkle!

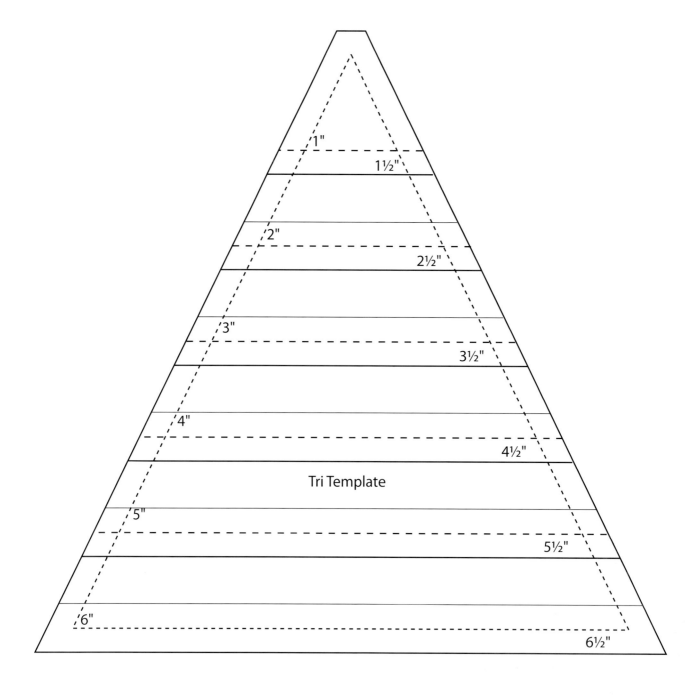

1"
1½"
2"
2½"
3"
3½"
4"
4½"
Tri Template
5"
5½"
6"
6½"

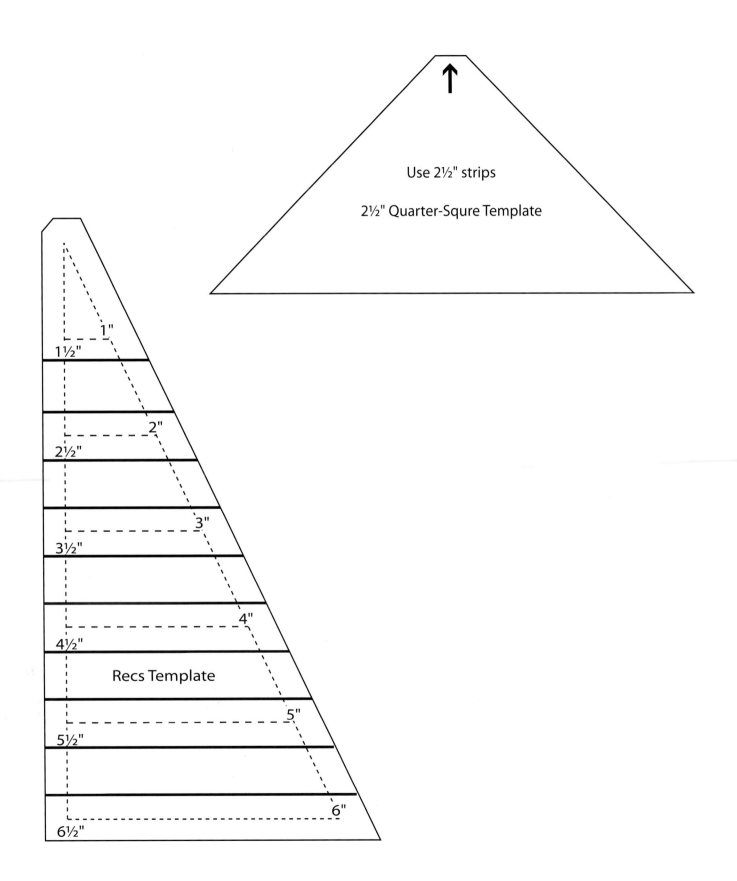

Use 2½" strips

2½" Quarter-Squre Template

1"

1½"

2"

2½"

3"

3½"

4"

4½"

Recs Template

5"

5½"

6"

6½"

RESOURCES & CONTRIBUTORS

EZ Flying Geese Ruler (formerly called Easy Star & Geese Ruler)
EZ Jelly Roll Ruler
EZ Hearts Cut Tool
EZ Pineapple/Log Cabin Ruler
You can order these tools directly from me on my website:
www.kimberlyeinmo.com

It is with sincere appreciation I would like to thank the following companies for their support of products and services that helped make this book possible. The fabric, batting, tools, and supplies featured or mentioned in this book are among my personal favorites and can be purchased at your local quilt shop, sewing machine dealer, on the Internet, or by mail order.

American Quilter's Society
My favorite publisher of this and other top quality quilting books
P.O. Box 3290
Paducah, KY 42002-3290
Phone: 270-898-7903
Web: www.americanquilter.com

Aurifil
For generously providing threads
184 Shuman Blvd. Suite 200
Naperville, IL 60563
Phone: 312-212-3485
Web: info@aurifilusa.com

Clover Needlecraft Inc.
Sewing, quilting notions, and tools including Yo-Yo Makers!
13438 Alondra Blvd.
Cerritos, CA 90703
Web: www.clover-usa.com

Electric Quilt Company
EQ7 and other quilting software products
419 Gould Street, Suite 2
Bowling Green, OH 43402-3047
Phone: 419-352-1134
Web: www.electricquilt.com

Fairfield Processing Corp.
For generously providing all the batting: wool, cottong, and bamboo blend
P.O. Box 1157
Danbury, CT 06813-1157
Phone: 800-980-8000
Web: www.poly-fil.com

Jilily Studio Needle Arts
Appliqué glue
15083 Bugle Ridge Dr.,
Herriman, UT 84096
Phone: 801-234-9884
Web: www.jililystudio.com

Moda Fabrics/United Notions
For generously providing fabric
13800 Hutton Drive
Dallas, TX 75234
Phone: 800-527-9447
Web: www.unitednotions.com

Olfa-North America
Rotary cutters and blades
5500 N. Pearl St., Suite 400
Rosemont, IL 60018
Phone: 800-962-6532
Web: www.olfa.com

Pfaff USA
Sewing machine and accessories
SVP Worldwide
c/o Pfaff
P.O. Box 7017
LaVergne, TN 37086-7017
Web: www.pfaff.com

Prym Consumer USA, Inc.
Omnigrid rulers and cutting mats
P.O. Box 253
Burlington, WA 98233
Phone: 360-707-2828
Web: www.dritz.com/brands/
omnigrid/index.php

Robert Kaufman Fabrics
For generously providing fabric
129 West 132nd Street
Los Angeles, CA 90061
Phone: 800-877-2066
Web: www.robertkaufman.com

Rowenta USA
Irons and steamers
2199 Eden Road
Millville, NJ 08332
Phone: 800-ROWENTA
Web: www.rowentausa.com

Schmetz
Sewing machine needles
9960 NW 116 Way, Suite 3
Medley, FL 33178
Web: www.schmetz.com

The Simplicity Creative Group
TRI RECS Tools, quilting rulers, tools, and notions
6050 Dana Way
Antioch TN 37013
Phone: 800-545-5740
Web: www.ezquilt.com

Longarm Machine Quilting Services
Birgit Schüller
Creative BiTS
Schachtstrasse 5
66292 Riegelsberg
Germany
Phone: +49 (6806) 920 447
Email: birgit.schueller@
creativebits.biz
Web: www.creativebits.biz

Photography
Alisha Pergola Photography
Web: http://www.
alishapergolaphotography.com
Email: Alisha@
alishapergolaphotography.com

ABOUT THE AUTHOR

Kimberly Einmo is an author, designer, judge, tool designer, and international quilting instructor. Her books have all been published by the American Quilter's Society including *Quilt a Travel Souvenir*, *Jelly Roll Quilts & More*, and *Jelly Roll Quilt Magic*. Kimberly's original quilt designs and numerous articles have appeared in a wide variety of publications. Her classes and mystery quilt series are in high demand by students everywhere. Most recently, she has an online video series at www.craftsy.com, called *Magic Jelly Roll Quilts*.

To date, Kimberly is the only instructor invited to represent the United States at the Annual Prague Patchwork Meeting where she was the featured speaker in 2008, 2010, and 2012. Kimberly is part of an elite group of sewing professionals who represent BERNINA and Pfaff, and she loves to share her passion and enthusiasm for quilting with people everywhere.

Kimberly has been married to Kent, a retired Air Force officer, for more than twenty-three years. They have two sons, Joshua and Andrew. To complete their family, they have one very pampered pooch, Divot, and two exceptional cats, Tuffy and Snickers, who can be found in her studio keeping Kimberly company (adding fiber content to her quilts: 80% cotton, 20% cat hair).

MORE AQS BOOKS

This is only a small selection of the books available from the American Quilter's Society. AQS books are known worldwide for timely topics, clear writing, beautiful color photos, and accurate illustrations and patterns. The following books are available from your local bookseller, quilt shop, or public library.

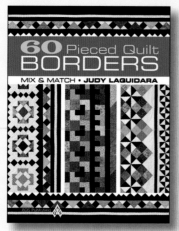

#8662 $26.95

#8523 $26.95

#8665 $19.95

#8664 $19.95

#8146 $26.95

#8663 $24.95

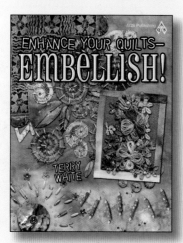

#8532 $26.95

#8529 $26.95

#8349 $24.95

LOOK for these books nationally.
CALL or VISIT our website at

1-800-626-5420
www.AmericanQuilter.com